# POINTE PATROL

## HOW NINE PEOPLE (AND A DOG) SAVED THEIR NEIGHBORHOOD FROM ONE OF THE MOST DESTRUCTIVE FIRES IN CALIFORNIA'S HISTORY

## EARIK BEANN

**Profoundly**[1]
PUBLISHING

ISBN: 978-1-7327408-2-2 (ebook)

ISBN: 978-1-7327408-3-9 (paperback)

*What follows is a true story, although I have taken the liberty of changing people's names and other small details to protect their privacy. Most of these events have been seared into my memory and were easy to remember. Other parts had to be pieced together after the fact. Having said that, I've discovered that my memory isn't nearly the iron trap that I once thought it was, so I apologize in advance for any mistakes or omissions I may have made.*

# SANTA ROSA EVACUATION MAP
# Tubbs Fire, October 2017

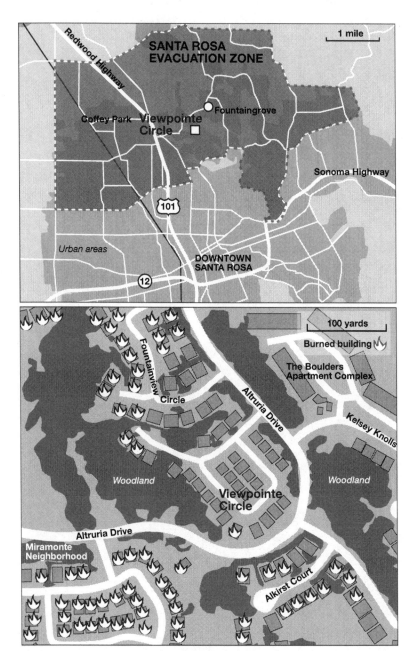

# CHAPTER 1

# Fire!

I WAS ASLEEP when the doorbell rang. I rolled over and lifted up my phone to see the time. It was 1:30 in the morning. I had been having trouble sleeping and had already been up three times that night: once because Oscar woke me up to take him out to pee, once to close the umbrella on the deck to protect it from the crazy wind that had picked up, and once to shut the windows against the heavy smoke smell that was making it hard for me to sleep.

Laura rolled over and mumbled something, still half asleep. "I think there's someone at the door," I told her, swinging my feet out over the edge of the bed to get up.

It was obvious that Oscar hadn't heard the bell, or he'd have already been down the stairs and by the door. The average Doberman doesn't like strangers, and they can be very protective of their homes and people. Oscar, being bred from a working line, tends to have even stronger reactions than average. Usually he hurls himself against the door from the inside, furiously barking and growling until I can grab him and drag him off to his kennel. After having accidentally been bitten when I got between him and a FedEx delivery person years ago, he is no longer allowed to meet or interact with anyone waiting at the entrance. But tonight, for some reason, he hadn't heard the bell and wasn't reacting, so I managed to walk out of the bedroom and close the door behind me before he got up to follow.

If you think about it, there can be almost no good reason for anyone to be at the door that time of night, and I wasn't sure if it would be wise to open it without at least having some idea of what was going on outside. There's a landing halfway down the stairs between our bedroom and the ground floor, with a tall window that runs all the way up the length of the house. The shade was down, and I moved it sideways to peek out.

The first thing I saw was Elliot, from the house across the street. He was outside in boxer shorts and an undershirt, walking somewhere off to the left. *What was Elliot doing outside in his underwear?* I could hear lots of commotion outside—doors slamming and cars driving by—but the strangest was the peculiar sound of many horns honking from somewhere far away. Between all the activity and the smell of smoke, I guessed that the police or fire department was here. *Was there a fire?*

I continued down the stairs and opened the door but was surprised to find nobody there. I made my way out into the street, trying to figure out what was going on. The winds were strong, and the smell of smoke was intense. It smelled the same as when I had found myself standing on the wrong side of a campfire on a windy day.

At that point I noticed Wayne, from the other side of the circle. There is only one way in and out of Viewpointe Circle, and the street is shaped like the letter *Q*, not counting the entrance. There are eight houses in the center of the circle arranged in two rows of four, and the rest of us form a ring around the outside of the street. There are four houses side-by-side down the tail of the *Q*, which dead-ends after the fourth house. Wayne lived in the house right at the entrance to the circle.

I never interacted with Wayne much, only having talked with him superficially at the monthly potlucks that our neighborhood threw. Potlucks usually make me feel awkward, so I tend to resist attending them, but Laura forced me to go to a few and try to connect. Each month a different person would volunteer to host, and there was often some sort of theme to make things interesting. Elliot had hosted a "tacky" party, where we drank cheap beer, ate hot dogs, and tried to guess which one of three kinds of boxed wine had actually won a best-in-class award. (Only three people actually got it correct, the rest of us incorrectly selected what basically amounted to crap wine, at least in the eyes of the wine snobs.) Norma, who lived on the other end of the center of the circle from Elliot, had been next, and hosted an Elvis-themed party, complete with a full-size cardboard cutout of the King, and music to match. Wayne, who worked with SWAT, was forced to leave Norma's party early, as he had been called in to deal with a double homicide in a town north of Santa Rosa.

Wayne came up to me in the street, noticeably agitated. He is very tall, with a strong, athletic body. He had been the first to notice the orange glow in the sky, having driven out of our circle and up the hill to find that fire was approaching us from two directions. He rushed home, told his wife to get ready to leave, and then started pounding on doors to wake all the rest of us up. A couple other neighbors had joined him as they learned the news, knocking on doors and making their way around the Q to let everyone know what was happening.

"Paradise Ridge is on fire," he told me, his eyes wild. "If you have to evacuate, head south or west. Don't go east or north. That's all I can tell you—I'm here as a neighbor and don't have any official information."

"OK. Thanks," is all I could think to respond, and I headed back inside. Although I've put what Wayne told me here in quotes, I later came to understand that I misunderstood him. He didn't say *if* I had to evacuate, but that I *should* evacuate. As in, get in your car and drive away, *right now*.

By now Laura was up and waiting at the top of the stairs to see what was happening.

"That was Wayne. He says there's a fire and that we might need to evacuate," I told her. We stood there and looked at each other for a minute.

Here's the interesting thing about situations like this. Part of you doesn't want to accept the fact that something is actually wrong and decisive action needs to be taken, because the implications of what might happen in that case are pretty huge and, frankly, very inconvenient. Part of me just wanted to deny the whole thing and write Wayne off as being an overreacting Boy Scout. That part of me considered that maybe the best option was just to go upstairs and get back in bed, and let everyone else freak out for no good reason. I didn't see any way how a fire could really get to Viewpointe Circle. We were deep in the city. There was a lot between us and wherever a fire would be coming from, and even if a handful of houses got burned on the edge of the city, there was no way the fire department wouldn't be able to contain things before it got to us. It just didn't make any sense.

But what if this was for real? And exactly where was Paradise Ridge, anyway? I honestly didn't know how close that was, having only moved in a year ago and not being familiar with all the different subdivision names in the Fountaingrove area where we lived.

When you read stories of what happened on the *Titanic*, you'll come across similar reactions from the passengers as they were informed that the ship was sinking. Some of them just blew it off and went back to sleep, thinking that the whole thing was an overreaction. Others took it seriously and went up on deck to try to save their lives. I don't think any of the doubters lived to tell the story.

"OK. I'm going to pretend this is real and get ready, just in case," I said. Laura agreed, and then we had to figure out what exactly to take, which wasn't at all an easy process.

The first thing I did was go into the garage and get the two cat carriers for Peaches and Squatchie. They were brothers from the same litter, born in a barn in Tennessee. If you didn't know them well, it was hard to tell them apart, and a lot of people thought that we only had one tabby instead of two.

I found them sleeping on the couch, put each into his own carrier, and then set them by the door. Squatchie had run out the back door earlier that night, and Laura and I had to go looking for him in the dark. Ever since a cat of mine got eaten by a mountain lion in Colorado, we've always brought everyone in at night. We've actually trained them to come when they hear their dinner bell ringing, so there is always a way to get them if they're late or if there's an emergency. The first month we moved in, Squatchie climbed up some vines to someone's roof and got trapped for a week. Since then, he stays pretty close and is even easier to find—which is lucky for him, as he would have picked the worst possible night to stay outside if he hadn't come.

The next thing I got was Oscar's metal kennel, or *his cage* as we call it more commonly, and wrestled it down the stairs. "Oscar, go to your cage," is a phrase heard quite frequently at our place. The Schutzhund crowd that I trained with a couple years back thought it was the most hilarious command. If you've got a treat handy, and there's no FedEx guy lingering at the door, he'll run right in there without any trouble.

Right around this time the power went out, so all our preparations were being done by flashlight. When I was little, my dad had kept a huge blue Maglite flashlight by the side of his bed. He mounted it in clasps, so he'd always know exactly where it was and be able to get to it in the dark. It took four D-cell batteries, was waterproof, threw an amazing adjustable long-distance beam, and was completely overbuilt in all ways. He still has it now, over thirty years later. It made an impression on me, and so I've also got a nice blue Maglite in the bathroom, along with two others, and I've even put small ones in the cars. I'll probably get more of them one of these days soon, as backups if nothing else.

One of the cool things about that particular flashlight is that the base is flat, so you can stand it up easily on a table, turn it to wide beam, and completely illuminate a room. I had my blue one, and Laura had the spare, and between the two of us, we were able to deal with things hands-free despite it being dark otherwise.

When I say it was dark, I mean it was really, really dark. The smoke had been getting thicker by the minute and blocked out any moonlight that might have existed. I think those winds, which were the strongest I've seen in California in my three plus years living here so far, must have contributed by blowing the smoke sideways, right through our neighbor-hood. I learned that not everyone on the street actually owned flashlights, as I loaned my spares out to Pointe Patrol later on, so I don't know how other people managed to pack up in the dark. Probably by using their phones, I guess, which would work to illuminate a small room but not much else. Good luck chasing down a looter in the night using just your cell phone as a flashlight. But I'm getting ahead of myself.

I'll have to admit, I did get a little stumped on figuring out what to pack. We didn't have an emergency bag prepared and hadn't really put much thought into what we would need in a situation like this. It became difficult to prioritize what to take, as there are necessities such as clothes and medications to consider, but also items needed to run my business, like the computer, as well as sentimental things. Given only the space available in our two cars, including us and the animals, what gets taken and what gets left behind? And exactly how much time was there to figure it out?

The next thing after the animals ended up being our computers, both Laura's iMac and my PC. My whole business is run online, and although I have backups of everything available, having to restore it all would be a huge endeavor, especially if I made a mistake and found that my backups were incomplete or out-of-date. Laura is in a similar situation. So the next things to get carried down the stairs were a bunch of computer parts on my end, as well as Laura's iMac.

Let me stop here and just vent a little bit about that box that Apple provides with their iMacs. We've moved around a lot the last few years, so we saved that box for times when Laura's computer needs to be packed. It's a very clever design that opens up to hold the entire computer and all the peripherals. Unfortunately, it's a little too clever for its own good in an emergency.

It's not a rectangle, and it's smaller at the top than it is at the base. So to get the computer in there, you have to take out the three or four Styrofoam pieces and arrange them properly so that it all closes up again in the correct way. And you don't know if you've done it right until you get all the pieces in position around the computer and try to fit it in the box. It's kind of like a puzzle, since there's only one way to do it, and if you get it wrong, the box won't close. I've never had an issue putting it together before, but trying to get that stupid box assembled in the middle of the night by flashlight, with a fire bearing down on me, along with the mounting stress of time pressure against me, was a completely frustrating experience. Imagine trying to put a kid's puzzle together while at the same time being charged by a grizzly bear. I don't think a lot of people are going to be able to accomplish that task, especially if they get thrown into the situation with no warning. That's a lot like how this felt.

In the moment, it actually reminded me of my wedding, which is kind of a strange thing to say. Like most couples do, Laura and I had a place in the ceremony where we were going to exchange rings. The time came, and my best man handed me Laura's ring. All I had to do was take it and put it on her finger.

Easy, right? Like, so easy that it wouldn't even cross your mind ahead of time to think there would be some sort of problem. But standing up on that stage on my wedding day, saying vows, and being witnessed by the 120 closest people to me, I found that my motor skills were just not up to that most basic of tasks. I couldn't actually get the ring between my fingers in any kind of secure way, and if I forced it, I knew it would slip and I'd drop it. The last thing I wanted to do was drop the ring and then have it bounce under something. Then we'd have to stop, and everyone would have to get on their hands and knees to search. And what if one of those diamonds chipped on the way down? Or what if it fell down a floor grate? Not a good way to start out a marriage! This is what I was thinking as I fumbled with that ring, trying to figure out how to get a hold of it so I could just put it on her. In the end, my solution was just to leave it flat on my hand and sort of scoop it onto her waiting finger. Not the smoothest of moves, but infinitely better than the alternative. Add enough stress and nerves to any situation, and simple tasks can become quite difficult.

So that's how it was with that computer box, although I finally got it all buttoned up in the end. I'll freely admit that I cussed Apple out the whole time I struggled with it, and Laura did have to come in and talk me down once or twice.

As things got carried to our staging pile downstairs, I'd sort through and take loads out to the car. Each load became more difficult than the last, because conditions outside were rapidly deteriorating. Every time I'd step out the door I found myself in a swirling maelstrom of ash. I couldn't keep my eyes open, because it stung to look anywhere. So I'd squint my way to the car, throw whatever items I had in as fast as I could, and run back into the house. I'd then come inside, dust myself off, and comment about how bad it was out there and how strangely dark things were getting. It became clear very quickly that the cars really needed to be loaded sooner rather than later, because things were just *not right* outside, and it was getting harder to function out there with every passing moment. If we waited, we might not get a chance to take everything we wanted.

The loading process was eventually completed, with both cars being packed and ready to go. The animals were the only thing we hadn't loaded yet—the cats were sitting in their carriers by the door, and Oscar was resting at our feet. Laura and I sat in the two chairs downstairs by the front door, just waiting and talking. Again, we were under the mistaken impression that someone from the fire department was eventually going to come and officially tell us to leave, having misunderstood that Wayne had already done that an hour and a half earlier.

I'm not sure what it was that finally made us go. Things were now pretty smoky inside the house, even though all the windows were shut tight. There was also that tingling feeling when your intuition is trying to get your attention. We both felt it. Laura turned to me and said, "We should probably just go." I was about to suggest the exact same thing to her.

The front room where we were sitting is the largest in our house, with tall cathedral ceilings and lots of windows. We are both attracted to religious art, so there's an eclectic collection from many different spiritual traditions in that room. One of our largest pieces is a life-size brass statue of Shiva, one of the gods from Hindu mythology, depicted doing an ecstatic dance. Between him and the stone pedestal that we have him up on, that statue weighs over 800 pounds and has caused all sorts of trouble for anyone who has ever tried to move it.

As I got ready to open the front door, I paused and waited quietly as I saw Laura go over to that statue and kneel down in front of it. She reached out to the pedestal with both her hands and bowed her head, saying a silent prayer. She remained still for a few moments, in stark contrast to the wind and ash that was raging on the other side of the front door. In the space between where I stood and where she knelt, I could see the haze from the smoke that had found its way into our house. When she was finished, we smiled at each other and left.

The cats went into Laura's car, and Oscar went into his kennel in the back of mine. He took longer to load, so Laura was about a minute ahead of me when I pulled out. The plan was to head south and meet up at a gas station in Rohnert Park, which is the next town below Santa Rosa on Highway 101.

As I pulled out of the circle, I was stunned again by how dark things were. It reminded me of trying to drive through blizzards in Colorado, where I grew up. My lights were on, but I couldn't see very far. So much smoke!

I had the fleeting thought that maybe it would be fun to take a video on the way out, to show how things looked, but I only got about a second recorded before I changed my mind. I didn't want to be distracted, and I didn't have a way to hold the phone up without using my hand. The video didn't look like anything anyway—just driving in the dark, basically.

I made it up toward Fountaingrove Parkway, the main street out of the subdivision to the north. There's a golf course there, right across from the stop light. It was on fire. All the trees on the course were burning. *Holy shit! This is real!*

I didn't wait for the light to turn green. I turned left, heading down the hill toward 101. The unusually strong winds that we had experienced that night had done some damage. Tree branches had fallen onto the road earlier and would suddenly materialize out of the darkness in front of me. I swerved around them. I then drove past a burning structure, flames leaping out its sides.

I made it down to the big four-way stop at Mendocino, which ran next to Highway 101, and stopped at the light. The fancy hotel to the right, where Laura and I had considered going for Christmas dinner a couple years ago, was burning. Across the street and to the left was Journey's End mobile home park. Journey's End was on fire. Not just one or two homes, but the entire park was just completely engulfed in flames. Someone was standing there on the corner watching it. There were other people running across the street. I wasn't sure where they were going, or what they were trying to do. They didn't seem like they were in trouble.

Traffic lights had become suggestions, not rules. I drove forward. I could feel the heat coming from Journey's End penetrating through my car door from all the way across the street. It was hot.

*Fuck! Where were the police? Where was the fire department?* Santa Rosa was burning down, and there was no one around.

Laura called my phone. "Hey! Where are you!? Should I get on 101?"

I was just driving across the overpass to get onto 101 South myself. I looked down and could see that the highway was on fire, too. The grass in the middle and on the sides was burning, along with some of the signs and the wooden posts holding up the guardrails. Amid all of this, the highway was getting backed up with people escaping from the north.

"No! Don't get on 101!" I had put her on speaker, with my phone sitting in the cup holder between the seats. I recognized her car ahead of me. She was stopped at the top of the on-ramp. There was a car between us, which dodged around her to get on the highway. "It's me behind you. Back up and follow me. Let's take the side roads."

We then took a left, down the street that ran parallel to 101 South on the other side, running a red light. We left our phones connected so we could talk the whole way.

"How much gas do you have?" I asked.

"About half a tank."

There was less than a quarter tank in my car. I estimated I could go about sixty or seventy miles. That was enough to get to safety, although I really wished I had filled it up when I had a chance the day before.

We passed a large delivery or moving truck—I couldn't tell which—that had pulled off at an angle into a parking lot on the right. It was burning, with flames eating the side toward us. I could imagine the driver barreling into the lot on fire, ditching the truck and running away on foot.

"Wow. This is straight out of a disaster movie," I commented.

"I know!"

"OK, I don't think we should go on the highway." We could see it to our left, and it was crowded. I don't like crowded highway driving in good conditions. I definitely wasn't interested in sitting in gridlock during a firestorm.

"All of these people are going to need hotels," Laura said. "I'm not sure if we're going to find a place in Rohnert Park." That would mean we'd have to go even farther south.

"San Rafael? Novato? But I don't have a ton of gas. It's going to take hours to get to either one of those if the traffic is like this the whole way. Should we head west?"

We decided to head toward Sebastopol. It's a small town about fifteen minutes to the west where we had taken some Spanish lessons a few months ago. We liked it and had even considered moving there at one time but could never find a place to rent. We knew how to get there on back roads without driving on any highways, which gave us a chance to skirt around potentially congested areas.

We came to a point where we needed to turn right. There was a gas station on the corner, and they were open. I saw a woman go inside. I looked down at my fuel gauge and considered stopping to fill up, but I could still see flames here and there, which made me nervous. *Maybe just get out of town first.*

As we had moved deeper into the city, the traffic had increased, and there were as many cars around now as if it had been 3:30 in the afternoon instead of the morning. Someone ahead of me cut through the gas station's parking lot to avoid having to stop at the light ahead.

We turned right, which would take us to the western edge of Santa Rosa. We'd then be able to make our way south, almost to Highway 12, and then take the back roads over to Sebastopol. What we didn't realize at the time is that this took us right into the path of all the people evacuating Coffey Park.

Like Fountaingrove, Coffey Park was burning. The fire had jumped the highway and gotten into their neighborhood. It was a working-class suburb, and the houses were closer together, which meant the fire spread faster and took houses down like dominoes. Unlike us, who had been given hours of time to figure out what to pack, many Coffey Park residents had to evacuate immediately wearing only whatever they had on their backs. Weeks later, I talked to one couple in the grocery store who described driving away from their house half-dressed, with the back end of their pickup truck on fire. As they left, houses exploded in flames on either side of them as if they were in a disaster movie. Not everyone made it out.

As cars flooded into the road from Coffey Park, things began to move slowly. People who lived in the apartments along the way came out and were standing on the sidewalk in their pajamas, looking around and wondering what was going on.

Someone made a move to cut in front of Laura from the other lane, but she pulled up to block. She rolled her window down and shouted, "That's my husband!" pointing at me, and the driver backed off and merged behind her instead. I heard Peaches and Squatchie meowing in the background on the phone. They don't like car rides.

I was actually very impressed about how cool people were handling the drive, given the fact that they were fleeing for their lives. The traffic lights were all flashing red, so we took turns at intersections, but we'd go three cars at a time rather than the usual one. It was faster that way. I only saw one person driving erratically in a shoulder, but they eventually calmed down and went with the flow like everyone else. People let each other in when needed, and I don't remember hearing any honking or seeing any rude behavior.

The only close call I really had on the drive was when Laura almost rear-ended me at one point due to being distracted. She was driving close, and there was a lot going on, so it was understandable. I didn't see any accidents, but I'm not sure if anyone would have stopped and pulled over had they been in a minor fender bender anyway. I certainly wouldn't have. Not under those circumstances.

At some point, our call dropped, and Laura and I weren't able to reconnect right away. But I could see her out the back, and she was riding my tail, so it wasn't an issue. We both knew where the other was.

When we eventually reconnected, she informed me that she had called Judith, and we were heading to her house. Judith is a longtime friend of Laura's, who she has known for over twenty years. She lives alone in Graton with Sunshine, her Goldendoodle, and a pack of cats (not all hers) that she takes care of. We had been to her house for Christmas dinner with her sons and had stayed with her when we first came out from North Carolina to look for a house. One of the reasons why we had taken those Spanish lessons in Sebastopol was so all three of us could do something fun together. So she was a logical choice as far as someone who might take us in during an emergency. The big problem was that she was scared of Oscar. She had to take a Xanax the first time she met him when she came out to visit us in Napa, where we first landed when we moved to California, and although she met him a number of times since then without issues, it was always stressful for her. It was probably our fault. We told her too many stories about the crazy things he'd done in the past. Incidentally—and I didn't know this at the time—our old house in Napa was at that very moment burning to its foundation for the second time in forty years, consumed by the Atlas Fire.

Graton is a tiny town. Fewer than two thousand people live there. It's just past Sebastopol, so we were heading the right direction and didn't need to make any route changes. As we made our way out of Santa Rosa and into more rural and undeveloped areas, I was struck by the immense orange glow off to my right that lit up the sky. Some people had stopped on the side of the road and gotten out of their cars to look at it and take pictures. I had an urge to do the same, although I didn't, but I did slow down quite a bit as I took it all in. When witnessing that kind of display of nature's power, you can't help but feel a certain sense of awe and wonder. It was beautiful. Terrible, but beautiful. This wasn't something you got to see every day, or every lifetime.

# CHAPTER 2

# Holy Crap, What Just Happened?

IT WAS ALMOST 5 a.m. when we pulled into Judith's driveway. I let Oscar out to pee, and then put him back in his kennel in the back of the car. He was going to have an awkward day.

Judith had been up since Laura had first called her, and she had coffee brewing and the news on. She could smell the smoke on us as soon as we walked through the door.

We put the cats in her library, which has glass doors that allow it to be closed off from the rest of the house. Sunshine would chase them otherwise, and it was best to keep them contained in a place they weren't familiar with.

We caught up with Judith and told her our story, trying to get our bearings and figure out the bigger picture. The entire Fountaingrove area and a section of the neighborhoods across 101 to the west of it had been declared a mandatory evacuation zone.

Multiple dangerous fires had erupted across both Napa and Sonoma counties, quickly growing out of control and threatening everything in their paths. The fire that we had evacuated from was the Tubbs Fire, named after a street in Calistoga where it began. Fanned by near hurricane winds, it traveled at the rate of an acre a minute and threw burning embers out up to a mile ahead. It only took four hours for it to move the twelve miles from Calistoga to Santa Rosa, across rural areas, over the top of a mountain range, and through a forest, to finally barrel full speed into Fountaingrove like some diabolical freight train that had gone horribly off the tracks.

For some reason, I harbored the mistaken idea that I'd still be able to get a little sleep that day. I was still too worked up from the night's events, and part of me kept trying to listen to the news blaring in the other room. When I heard Fountaingrove mentioned, I gave up the idea of getting any sleep, got some coffee, and joined Laura and Judith by the TV. They both seemed to be working through their second and third cups already.

The reporter was interviewing a man on Ranchette Road, back in Santa Rosa, whose house had burned down. Before we lived in our current place, we had spent four months right across the street from Ranchette Road. In fact, I had taken Oscar on many walks there. I recognized the guy they were interviewing. I wasn't friends with him but frequently waved to him on my walks. I knew right where he lived. I even knew what kind of car he drove. His house was gone. All the houses were gone, all the way down the whole street. All burned to the ground.

That man on TV, who I knew well enough to recognize, but not well enough to name, was talking about how long he'd been there and how he planned to rebuild. He actually had quite an upbeat attitude, all things considered. I could see his neighbors wandering around behind him, trying to take in the fact that their homes were destroyed. It was strange seeing that on TV. We've all watched disasters on the news, but seeing one happen on a street you know, and to people you recognize, isn't something you ever expect. That sort of thing is supposed to happen to *other* people. I never thought it would happen to *me*. It's a surreal feeling when you find yourself right in the middle of it.

Then, the news moved to another reporter, showing some of the houses that had survived in Coffey Park. "These residents felt lucky that their houses had survived the fires in Santa Rosa, where just across the street their neighbors lost everything. But it wasn't all good news for them, as hours before they returned, looters had broken into their homes." *Looters? At a time like this!?* I couldn't believe that anyone would stoop that low. Neither could the news anchor, once the reporter signed off. "Looters? Oh, my gosh," he said. "If you are doing that, just knock it off. Right now." Fire is tragic, but it's not personal. Looters are. Looters are a violation.

I was almost certain that we had just lost everything in the fire. If someone had asked me the odds, I'd have put them up at around ninety-five percent. One neighborhood after another around us made its way onto the television screen, and they were all completely devastated.

Laura and I have bad luck with houses. Seven years ago, we had to sell our house in Colorado, due to issues that could be traced back to the 2008 financial crisis. At the time, we treated it as sort of an adventure and packed everything up and moved 1,200 miles to a rental property in rural Tennessee. We might as well have moved to another country, given how different things were between those two states. After a year, we were forced to move again and landed in North Carolina. The pattern continued, and every year, the landlord would decide to sell the property rather than extend the lease to us, one after another, over and over. This was our seventh house in as many years. We liked all of them except for one, where the landlord used to like to sneak in and look around when we were out of town, but we had just never been able to stay in any of them longer than a year. It was like the Universe would not allow us to put down any roots. We were tumbleweeds, constantly rolling in the wind without ever finding a place to land.

I thought the Viewpointe house was going to be different. We had just negotiated a two-year extension and signed the contract weeks ago. Finally, it was a chance to stay and just *be* somewhere for a change. A chance to try to slow things down and figure out how to pull our finances together to buy our own place. But now, the house was probably gone, and all our stuff with it. All our worldly possessions fit neatly into the back seats of two cars. We were homeless. And so were a ton of other people. The rental market in Sonoma hadn't been pretty to start with. What would it look like now with Fountaingrove and Coffey Park gone? In one night, Santa Rosa had lost five percent of its housing stock.

Move along, tumbleweed. But to where? And how long do I have to keep rolling? I formed a vague plan that day, and it consisted of basically getting in the car, pointing it south, and driving somewhere that wasn't on fire. Anywhere. Perhaps some people are not meant to settle, to own a home, or to have long-term friends and neighbors. How had that fate become my own?

We spent the morning watching the news and checking our phones. My sister called to make sure we were all right once she heard what had happened. Others were in touch via text. The cats had made themselves at home in their room and began to amuse themselves by knocking Judith's lamps off her tables and onto the ground. Yes, those cats actually *had* grown up in a barn.

When I went outside to check on Oscar, who was spending his day alternating between short walks and naps in the car, I noticed a white SUV parked across the street. As I approached, I could see that there was fire damage all along the driver's side. There was a brown spot that stretched over the hood and all the way down the side where the heat had discolored the finish and warped the metal. There were dark brown bubbles in the paint. Most striking was the fact that the headlight on that side had melted and then cooled, resetting into a strangely deformed version of itself that looked a lot like melted cheese. I was reminded of the heat I felt through the door as I drove past Journey's End. *What had this person driven through to get here?*

I took a picture and sent it off to friends and family. I had a feeling that a lot of people out of state didn't really understand how extreme the situation was and were playing it down in their minds. Pictures of melted headlights might help give them some context. I would see a lot worse in the coming days.

I made a mental note to try to watch for whomever it was that owned that SUV to get their story, but I never got the chance, as it was gone a few hours later.

At around midday, Laura made an announcement. "Tomorrow, I'm going to go to a shelter and volunteer to help. I'm not going to just sit around watching the news all day doing nothing!"

Two years ago, we had been in Napa when the big earthquake had hit. We were up on Atlas Peak, on top of tons of granite, so although we felt it, nothing bad happened because of it. There was no damage to our house, and aside from losing power, you would never know the city had just been through a magnitude 6.0 earthquake.

But down in the valley, things were much worse. Downtown was trashed. Houses were destroyed. I talked to one guy who told me that all of his kitchen appliances—his refrigerator, stove, and dishwasher—all decided to come out and do a tango together in the middle of the kitchen. The refrigerator opened both its doors, expelled all of its contents into the room, and then closed the doors again. Drawers opened and plates fell from shelves. If something was breakable, it got broken.

This is what other people were dealing with. We had no idea, being up on the hill and never having been through an earthquake before, so we just waited for things to get back to normal and went about our lives. We didn't know how lucky we had been. I think Laura always regretted that we didn't go down and help others clean up and had promised herself that if she ever had the chance to do it again, she'd make a different choice. Now was obviously her opportunity, and she wasn't about to lock herself away from people and get lost in the news cycle. I could understand her impulse. How much texting can you really do in a day anyway?

But, before making any plans, we had to find out once and for all whether or not our house had burned down. It wasn't enough to be ninety-five percent sure it was gone. We had to be certain. We wanted to see it with our own eyes and have that closure. We decided to drive back and find out, to take the opportunity to say goodbye to the parts of our lives that had burned there.

Before we left, we moved Oscar inside. Judith and Sunshine went and locked themselves in a back room, and then I brought Oscar and the kennel into the bedroom we were using. He went back in, thankfully without giving me too much attitude, although I knew he must be getting sick of being a cage dog, and then we closed the bedroom door and gave Judith the "all clear" so she could come back out.

Oscar was used to spending time in his kennel when we were gone, so it wasn't unusual for him. Years ago, we used to let him run free and guard the house, which would have been our preference all things being equal. But one day in North Carolina, we came back to find that he had managed to get up on the counter and knock down and break a mason jar filled with sunflower seeds. That in itself wouldn't have been such a big deal, but rather than being careful and just eating the sunflower seeds themselves, Oscar, being Oscar, ate all the broken glass, too. He threw up some of it, and I got cut through a paper towel just trying to clean it up.

When we took him to the emergency vet, they X-rayed him and pointed out all the shards of glass making their way through his system. I was surprised when the vet seemed mostly unconcerned. "I've seen dogs pass fish hooks. He should be OK as long as we're careful," he told us. They gave us some medicine, and sure enough, Oscar was fine after a couple days. But he didn't get left alone unattended much after that.

We took Laura's car and headed out. On the way out of town, we stopped to get gas. Hers wasn't as low as mine, but we weren't going to pass up the opportunity to fill up. People had been making runs on gas stations, and some of them had run out of their supply. The station we stopped at was completely out of the cheap stuff, only having premium available.

Normally, in a situation like this, you expect to see all kinds of price gauging and dishonorable behavior when it comes to buying things like gas or water. But I was shocked to see that this gas station had done the opposite. They had reduced the price of the premium gas to match what the regular had been before they ran out. They weren't in this to make a quick profit; they were helping people to be able to get gas. Sonoma County businesses really stepped up and did their part over the next few weeks. It was not the first time I found myself impressed.

We drove back on the highways, which was the fastest way. There was no need to wind our way through the back roads, as the traffic had eased. Everyone who had needed to evacuate from this direction had already done so.

We passed the K9 Activity Club on our way, which is where we board Oscar when we go out of town. We considered the possibility of moving him there now, to get him out of Judith's hair, but almost immediately decided against it. What if they needed to evacuate, too, and we weren't able to get him out in time? We were not going to put Oscar in a situation where he could potentially die in a fire without us being around to at least try to save him.

We drove up 101 toward the Bicentennial exit, which is the one that we take to get into Fountaingrove. As we got near, the traffic became more congested, and things began to move slowly. There were cones and a police car blocking the exit. They weren't going to let us in that way.

Unable to exit, we continued driving north, toward Windsor. We had been past some of this earlier in the morning during our evacuation. What we hadn't seen was how bad the destruction was just to the north of where we lived. Not only houses had burned, but businesses, too. An entire K-Mart and pizza place were charred shells of what they had been one day before, still smoldering. A gas station was gutted. The posts that held up the guardrails were even now still on fire, and the grass on the medians was black and burned. Here and there, emergency vehicles were driving around, trying to deal with things as best they could. It was obvious that the fire department had been overwhelmed.

The next exit was also blocked, so we had to keep driving north until we found a place to turn around. We weren't going to be able to get in from the highway. We needed to get closer, at least to a point where we could try to see our neighborhood. Viewpointe Circle is up on a hill, so we needed to find a spot close enough where we could see it or ask someone who might know what had happened to it.

We went back the way we had come, passing the burned-out K-Mart again, and made our way past all the blocked entrances. We then turned in and came up on Mendocino, which runs parallel to 101.

There are two ways into Viewpointe: either from Bicentennial or from Fountaingrove Parkway. Fountaingrove Parkway is the way we had driven this morning, and Bicentennial is one exit south. It's usually easiest to leave on Fountaingrove Parkway but to come back on Bicentennial.

There was a police line at Bicentennial, blocking the way up toward Viewpointe, as well as the way north to Fountaingrove Parkway. An older man dressed in a police uniform with the word "Volunteer" on his back was directing traffic to turn left to go across the overpass. We pulled off to the right, as close to him as we could get, and Laura got out. She thought she'd be able to explain the situation and talk him into letting us turn right and drive up to the house. After a few minutes, she came back, dejected.

"He isn't going to let us in," she said.

We pulled out and turned left, along with everyone else. But rather than giving up and leaving, we made a U-turn before we got to the overpass and found our way into a parking lot just across the street from the entrance to Bicentennial. It was an office building, but there were only a couple cars in the parking lot. Nobody was coming to work today.

"Come on," Laura said, and then got out.

Laura and I have different personalities when it comes to rules and authority figures. I'm much more of a rule follower and have a positive, respectful view of authority figures. Laura is the opposite. We are a good match in that respect, as long as the right one of us is handling the job at the time. The situation now was clearly more up her alley, and she led me across the street and cut through the parking lot of the bar on the corner of Bicentennial and Mendocino.

There were a lot of people standing around on the corner. I think they were either the press or volunteers. We didn't make eye contact with anyone while walking through the crowd, turning to make our way up the sidewalk on the other side of the police line, not looking back. Act like you have a reason to do what you're doing, and most people won't question it.

The way up to our house is completely uphill. It would probably be about a fifteen-minute walk if we pushed it, which we were happy to make under the circumstances. We passed the entrance to Home Depot, which for some reason had a river of water flowing down it and into the gutter. I couldn't tell if that was on purpose or if something had broken. We passed through and turned up a steep hill toward Miramonte, the neighborhood just down the hill from Viewpointe Circle. We can see Miramonte from our bedroom window. We knew we'd have to go through there, then make a right and go up another steep hill on Altruria Street, which curves around the back side of Viewpointe Circle before arriving at the entrance on the opposite side from Miramonte.

As we started up the hill, a black SUV pulled up beside us. There was a "Press" card in the windshield.

"Do you two live here? Do you need a ride?" the reporter asked us after he rolled the window down. We explained what we were doing and accepted his offer, pushing our way through all the junk cluttering up his seats. He worked for the *LA Times* and had just arrived in Santa Rosa after driving from Los Angeles as soon as the story about the fire broke. He looked worn out, but he didn't have time to rest as he still needed to try to get a story before it got too dark. It looked like we might get to be that story.

"I'm actually not supposed to give anyone rides because of liability," he disclosed. "But tell me where to go."

We directed him up the road toward Miramonte. We could already see houses destroyed as we approached, and the full scale of what had happened became apparent as we turned in to where that neighborhood had been.

I used to walk Oscar through Miramonte all the time. Laura and I had come down and put "Find Squatchie!" missing cat flyers in each of these people's mailboxes when Squatchie had gotten lost a year ago. (The mailman had called us and told us to knock it off, as we weren't supposed to do that.) This was a neighborhood filled with children and young couples. There was one guy who collected motorcycles. I'd always have to watch for him so he wouldn't startle Oscar. There was another who used to take his cat on walks around the block. He would walk and the cat would follow, and together they'd slowly make their way. It had been a vibrant, active neighborhood, with its own special personality. Now, it was a pile of rubble.

The houses were reduced to ash, no signs left of whatever had been inside of them. The gas hadn't been shut off yet, so each lot spewed a constant jet of hissing flame into the sky, a striking reminder of what had just happened hours ago. Cars that had been parked in driveways or on the street had been burned by the radiant heat, their wheels turned to liquid metal. The press was up here, documenting the destruction.

"Wow. Miramonte is gone," Laura commented.

As we slowly drove through the street, making our way through the ruins of Miramonte, I glanced out the window on the passenger side. There, up the hill, bearing silent witnesses to the destruction below, stood a perfect row of little stucco squares.

"Laura! Look! Our house is still there!"

# CHAPTER 3

# Visiting Viewpointe

AS WE DROVE into Viewpointe Circle, we spotted Wayne lounging on the grass across the street from his own house, facing the entrance to the circle.

"That's the guy who went around pounding on doors to wake everyone up in the morning," I explained to the reporter. He parked, and Laura and I both got out. The reporter stayed in the car, doing something with his phone. I wasn't sure what and didn't really care.

We headed back over to Wayne, who was dressed in a brown uniform. He had a gun holstered at his side and was lying with his back on the grass, his knees up. He sat up as we got closer. Two fire trucks were parked in a line along the street behind him. Their engines were off, and exhausted firefighters were sleeping on people's lawns all around the trucks, fully dressed in their yellow protective gear. It was obvious that they had been working really hard all night and through the day.

"Hey," I said as we went up to Wayne. "Thanks for waking everyone up this morning."

"Yes," Laura agreed, "we really appreciate it. You saved the neighborhood!"

Wayne is a very outgoing person and has more than his fair share of showmanship and bravado. But in that moment, he was temporarily lost for words and started to tear up. I wasn't sure what he had been doing since I last saw him, but whatever it was, it had been intense. After having seen the destruction just outside our circle, it was clear that we had been spared from the same fate by a hair's breadth. It was enough to make even the toughest among us pause and take a breath.

"I didn't save the neighborhood," he said. "That was Dave." Dave is an older, heavyset neighbor who we had met a few times at the neighborhood parties. He had lived in the circle forever, probably since it was first built. I hadn't talked with him much, but he had always been very friendly and sweet to both of us whenever we had interacted with him. What I hadn't known was that Dave was a retired firefighter, with almost four decades of experience.

"I knocked on his door and told him to evacuate, but he just said 'No, I'm not ready yet.'" Wayne continued, acting out his interaction with Dave, speaking both sides of the conversation and lowering his voice for Dave's part.

"'There's a fire coming from two directions! We've got to evacuate the neighborhood!'

'No, not ready yet.'

'What do you mean you're not ready!? I was just up the hill and saw the fire, motherfucker! You've got to go!'

'No, not ready yet.'

'Fine!'

"So I left him. He wasn't going to give up on his house without a fight. He stayed the whole day, putting out fires himself. When he ran out of water, he used a shovel to throw dirt and did whatever else he could to keep the fire away from the houses. He saved us. Dave is *The Man*."

"Wow!" was about all either of us could think to say in response.

"Being a police officer, I've seen what happens next. I'm going to stay the whole night and watch the entrance and make sure no looters come in here. I'll probably get a sleeping bag and sleep right here on the grass." The gun and police outfit made more sense after he said that.

"You think looters will try to get in here?" Laura asked. We both remembered the reports of looters from what we had heard on the news earlier in the day.

"After the evacuation, there were a ton of people that came through on ATVs and dirt bikes. All kinds of them, just driving up and down and all over the place. Somehow, they made their way in through little ways and cracks in the fence. Then Oakland PD came and just swarmed the area, and they all went away. It was actually pretty cool."

Evidently, a lot had been happening here while we had been gone. Directly across the street, in front of Wayne's own house, there were coolers, cases of bottled water, and various boxed snacks stacked in a huge pile. It was all put out on the street, along with a garbage can.

Wayne gestured to the pile and explained, "I put that out so any first responders can come and take a break if they need it. It's free for anyone back here."

Wayne looked over at the reporter, who was still in his car messing around with something. "Who's that guy?" he asked.

"He's a reporter," I answered. "He gave us a ride up. We told him you knocked on all the doors. He's probably going to want to talk to you."

Wayne made an affirmative gesture as if to say "Fine" but didn't seem enthusiastic about talking to any journalists. He didn't like the media. He thought they were all too liberal and were unfairly biased against the police. He vehemently hated the local paper and refused to read it after they had printed what he felt were completely one-sided articles involving past police shootings that he had inside knowledge of. His position was that California was full of too many "Libtards," who made impractical decisions based on emotion and not logic. He had tried to talk his wife into moving to a different state but had been unable to convince her.

We all said goodbye, and Laura and I made our way over to our own house. The reporter had gotten out of his car and caught up with us.

We all went inside, and everything was exactly how we had left it. It smelled like smoke, worse than we had remembered, but more importantly, everything was still there.

Laura went upstairs, and the reporter and I went out to the back deck. The side and back fences had burned. The fence on the left side was half gone, and I couldn't even see the one on the right side. The one directly behind us down the hill toward Miramonte was made of wood and wire, and the wood part was still on fire. I could see some small flames as what was left of the top boards were burning on both ends. The fountain below was blackened, and the two big potted plants we had near it didn't look like they made it. The first, a small palm tree, was bent in half and no longer had any green on it. The second, a peach tree, no longer had a pot. There was a circle of melted plastic around the dead tree; the soil still in the shape of the pot that had held it. The fire had burned the pot right out from under it. I was sad to see the peach tree go. We had brought it with us in two moves, and it had given its first harvest just this summer. The peaches had been small and bland, but that was to be expected since it was still young. I had eaten a couple of them anyway just because it was my own tree.

"How are you feeling, looking at all this?" the reporter asked me. He had pulled out his notepad and recording device. "Is this stunning? Apocalyptic?" He was trying to prompt me for the story he wanted me to tell him, and I felt a little like he was trying to put words in my mouth. I gave him some noncommittal answers and was glad when Laura showed up.

"I'm going to go put the fire out in the backyard," I said. As far as ways to excuse oneself from a boring conversation, that's a pretty hard line to beat. I made my way down from the deck and looked over at the right side of the house by the peach tree. The side fence was completely gone, having burned all the way up to the front gate, which was black and swung open on its hinges. What was left of the fence had collapsed in a pile on the narrow walkway by the side of the house. All the plants that had been growing along the fence, including one huge creeping vine, were gone. The neighbor's garbage cans, which sat on the other side of the fence, had melted from the heat and had huge gaping holes in their fronts. I didn't see any damage to either of our houses though, which was good.

Our backyard is on a steep hill, so it's terraced and has a path that winds down in a big *C* shape. I followed this, making my way to the burning fence at the bottom. I loosened the hose from its hanger and was glad to see good water pressure out of it. I began to put out the fire on the fence and doused the smolders in some of the lower flower beds nearby as well.

I pulled out my phone to text my parents and tell them that the house was still standing, holding it in one hand while I continued spraying with the other. I saw the reporter make his way down, wanting to take my picture.

"Can you put the fire out, and hold your phone up, but then look back past me over your shoulder?" he asked. I complied, and he took a picture, using the camera on his phone.

He frowned. "Don't smile. Look serious." He was still looking for the wrong kind of emotions out of me. If you want to write a story about heartbreak after a fire, you're probably better off interviewing someone whose house has burned down rather than someone whose house has miraculously survived. But I didn't say that and gave him my best stern look so he could take his picture.

After being satisfied with my drenching of the fence and surrounding areas, I took a better look around and thought I saw smoke coming from Joe and Carmen's yard two doors down. Theirs was the first house down the tail of the *Q* that formed Viewpointe Circle. Laura was up on the deck, texting people the news, and I told her I was going over there to check things out.

Joe and Carmen were the first neighbors we had met when we had moved in, and it hadn't been under the best circumstances. It was Squatchie's fault.

Back when we lived in Tennessee, we had rented a funky house out in the woods. It had a lot of character and we loved it, but it also had some downsides. One of them was that it was covered in brown recluse spiders. There must have been a hundred of them in there. As soon as I'd catch one and flush it down the toilet, two more would appear. I used to meditate downstairs, and before I'd sit down on my cushion, I'd always lift it to check for spiders. There was invariably a brown recluse hiding underneath. No matter how many times I'd clear them out, one would always come back. It was a big problem—you really don't want to get bitten by a brown recluse.

As a solution to our pest issue, and for other reasons, we decided to get some kittens, which is how we found Peaches and Squatchie. They were born in a barn, in the middle of nowhere, to a very religious and salt-of-the-Earth family. Their momma showed up one day, moved herself into Thaddeus's barn, and had her litter. Thaddeus and Bethany adopted her and put an ad out on Craigslist for the kittens. We brought them home, and within weeks, our spider problem was history. The kittens were like critter vacuums and would kill and eat anything that moved, including poisonous spiders. Pound for pound, house cats are the ultimate predator. They're pretty much the deadliest thing nature has figured out in all these eons of evolution, at least if you don't count tool-users like humans.

Since we got the cats, we had never lived in the city and always ended up on acreage. So they grew up mostly outside, only coming in at night. They look almost identical but have different personalities. Peaches is the lover, and Squatchie is the fighter. I've seen Sqautchie chase two foxes at once out of the yard and have witnessed him get into a huge fight with one in our driveway. He and that fox were moving so fast that I couldn't really see what was happening—just a rotating ball of fur and angry growls. It was like an animal kung fu battle. Back in Napa, he got into a fight with a rattlesnake. I broke that one up with a broom, so it was a tie—everyone lived. He has killed and eaten full-size squirrels. And through all of that rough and tumble life, he has never had a scratch on him. He's a ball of muscle, teeth, and attitude. So tough! He's also very handsome.

When you take cats like that and bring them into the city, it can be a little difficult for whatever city cats might already be there. Viewpointe was the first house we had in a dense neighborhood, and so this was the first time the cats didn't have space. Within a week, I got a call from animal control, telling me that they had Squatchie. He had gone over to Joe and Carmen's deck and attacked and wounded their cat, Goldie. He had done so with enough ferocity that they assumed he was feral, so they trapped him and had him taken to the pound.

After getting our cat back, Laura and I went over to Joe and Carmen's. At first, we were angry, but then we were apologetic after finding out what happened to Goldie. We ended up working out a schedule with them where our cats would go out at certain times during the day and then come back in so Goldie could take a turn. In the process, we became friends and had gotten close enough that we could get into their house and do errands for them when they weren't home. We looked on them almost like our adopted California parents.

Since the fences were all down, getting over to Joe and Carmen's was easy—I just walked from my backyard over to theirs. There was smoke coming up from the ground by their deck. There were no visible flames, but there was definitely underground smoldering. If left unchecked, I knew it could easily start their deck on fire. I got up on their deck, grabbed their hose, and started spraying.

I had realized that most of our neighbors were probably in the dark about whether or not they still had a house, just as we had been. There was no way to know unless you came up here and looked, and that wasn't the easiest thing to do. So, while I was hosing the ground off, I pulled out my phone and sent off a message to the group text thread that Laura and I shared with Joe and Carmen for the purpose of managing the cats.

### Group Text: Joe, Carmen, Laura, and Earik

**ME:** Your house is ok

Joe's answer came back almost immediately.

**JOE:** R U there? Thank you so much 🖤😎

**ME:** Yes. Viewpointe mostly is ok

**ME:** Miramonte is gone

**JOE:** Stay safe 🙏

A couple minutes later, I added:

**ME:** Our backyard is burnt

**ME:** I'm putting the fire out in your backyard with your hose right now!

**JOE:** Thank you so much 😄 Be safe. Please let me know if it gets worse. Do you think we could return tomorrow morning?

Laura and I both replied at the same time:

**LAURA:** Probably won't have power yet.

**ME:** Yes. But no power. You may have to talk the cops into letting you in

Having felt good about telling Joe what was going on, I thought it would be a good idea to tell anyone else I had in my phone as well. Unfortunately, Elliot from across the street was the only other person I had set up as a contact. I realized that I had spent over a year in the neighborhood and only had two contacts. That's a rate of one every six months, and I'm giving myself the benefit of the doubt with Joe and Carmen, since that was more about the cats than me. This is what happens when introverts spend all their time working from home: social connections form at a glacial rate.

## Elliot

**ME:** Your house is ok

It took Elliot a couple minutes to reply.

**ELLIOT:** Thank you so much, are you back at your house?

**ME:** Yes

**ME:** Backyard still burning

**ELLIOT:** Your backyard? Get the firemen to put it out!!!

**ELLIOT:** How did you get back in?

It took me some time to respond. I had soaked the ground pretty well and didn't see any other hot spots. I made my way around Joe's house to check the other side. There was a lot of smoke coming from two big rocks in the nature area between his house and the next one over, but the hose didn't reach, so I had to put my thumb over the tip and try to spray water over whatever was burning there. It took a while to get the smoke to stop. I replied back to Elliot after everything seemed fine.

**ME:** Walked in. Reporter gave us a ride up. Laura is auda-cious 😆

**ME:** I'm hosing it off myself

**ELLIOT:** You guys rock. Please keep an eye on our house. I don't have enough clothes 😊🖤

I finished up at Joe and Carmen's and headed back. Laura felt the same urge as I had, and she had informed others about the state of their houses as well. The reporter had left to talk to Wayne.

"We probably should head back soon," I said. It was starting to get dark. As we were leaving, I looked over and spotted Dave, standing at the end of the street. He was observing the house on the corner that had burned to the ground. The houses on either side were still standing but had seen better days. Both had windows blown out from the heat, and the paint was discolored on the sides.

"Let me go talk to Dave first," I said. Laura was fine waiting since she wasn't finished with all her texting. I wasn't surprised that she had a much more extensive contact list than I did. I don't know whether or not I'd call her a social butterfly, but next to me she's practically a living, breathing Twitter account.

The house Dave was watching was still smoldering, and smoke made its way up through the cracks in the debris pile. It had been built on the hill, and most of what was left of it was now scattered halfway down toward Altruria, ten or twenty feet under where we were standing and looking at it. The smell was sharp and different from the campfire scent inside my house. It almost smelled like sulfur. Dave's usually silver hair was a little darker in places than I had remembered. He was covered in soot.

We shook hands.

"Welcome back," he said. "Are you going to stay?"

Before giving me a chance to answer, he continued. "Because if you do, don't expect to sleep. This is not a night to be sleeping. Any of these spot fires could flare-up, and the houses could go. This one only took fifteen minutes to burn," he gestured at the smoldering remains before us. "You don't want to be sleeping when something like that happens." The implication of what might happen should one decide to sleep was clear. Viewpointe had survived one night, but there was a chance it might not survive another. We weren't out of the woods yet.

I thought of Oscar, still locked in his kennel at Judith's house. "No, we're not staying. I have to deal with the dog," I told him.

We stood quietly for a few moments, looking over the ruins, and then I said goodbye and left, making my way back to my own house. I checked the door to make sure it was locked, and Laura and I made our way back to the entrance of the circle. The reporter was in his car, busy dictating his article into his phone. He didn't look up from his work as we passed.

We waved to Wayne and the firefighters as we left and headed out of the circle and back down Altruria. I grabbed my flashlight on the way out, as it was clear that we wouldn't make it back to the car by the time the sun set. The street lights were out; it was going to be a dark night. We moved at a brisk pace.

We passed through Miramonte and back down the hill toward the entrance to Home Depot. As we walked past the burned-out field there, I spotted a mouse, sitting a few feet away from the sidewalk. He had survived the fire, but he had absolutely nowhere to hide, as all the vegetation in the area was burned down to the roots. He just sat there in the soot, out in the open, seemingly in a state of shock and unsure of what to do with himself or which way to go. I shined my flashlight on him and pointed him out to Laura. We saw that the attention made him anxious, so we kept moving and left him alone. I hoped he would be OK. This was the day for both animal and human survivors to come out and take stock of their situation.

# CHAPTER 4

# We Return

WHEN WE GOT back to Judith's, we found her watching the news. She was glad to hear that our house had survived. Laura and I walked to a nearby restaurant for dinner and then turned in for the night. Oscar stayed with us in our room. The floors were hard, so I had moved Sunshine's bed in from the living room so he would have a place to sleep. It barely fit between the side of our bed and the wall. Through the bedroom door, I could hear the muffled sound of the television coming from the other room. We settled in for a fitful, yet very much appreciated, night of rest.

The next morning, we had a big decision to make.

"I think we should go back," Laura said.

"And stay there? In the evacuation area? It's still burning."

"Dave is all alone, and our house is still standing. We can't stay here, and there's nowhere else. We belong at home."

And so, for the first time in seven years, rather than being pushed along to another city, we were given the opportunity to stay in one. The house wasn't the same one as we had rented. It was covered in soot, smelled of smoke, and was surrounded by the smoldering remains of what had once been a beautiful neighborhood. There were dead bodies in some of those homes. But it was our house, at least for one more day, and sometimes the most important decisions are made one day at a time.

The plan was to leave Peaches and Squatchie with Judith in their room, the floor of which was now covered in an embarrassing amount of fur and litter. We asked her if she could feed them and scoop their box, and she had agreed. We got their food out of our bag and measured out a number of days of meals for them in plastic bags, so she would only have to grab a bag and empty it into their bowls. The cats weren't safe at our house right now. If we took them home and one of them escaped at the wrong time, it could be tragic. For now, they would be better off here in the library. But Oscar was definitely coming.

As we got ready and made plans, Laura began work on setting up a neighborhood text thread. She has a master's degree in social work, with an emphasis on community organizing, so finding ways to bring people together is second nature to her. Hardly anyone even knew that our neighborhood hadn't burned, let alone the effort that was being made to try to protect it, so we needed a way where we could all share information and communicate. A group text message was the perfect solution. Laura initially named it *Viewpointe Circle Neighbors*, but it didn't take long before it got converted to *#VIEWPOINTE STRONG*.

## #VIEWPOINTE STRONG

**LAURA:** This is the start of a group text for Viewpointe Circle neighbors. If you have neighbors' cell numbers, please send them to me so I can add them.

She had added the handful of neighbors she had contact information for to the thread and began reaching out and adding more.

We loaded Oscar into the back of my car and left, thanking Judith for her help. We left Laura's car with her and gave her the keys in case she needed to move it. Traffic wasn't too bad, aside from a bunch of people driving in from somewhere to the north. On our way out, we visited the same gas station we had been to yesterday. There was a line but not a long one, and I was glad to see that they hadn't run out of gas.

Getting back was simply a matter of retracing our steps from yesterday. We drove to the intersection of Bicentennial and Mendocino and then parked in the lot of the office building across the street. I parked somewhere visible, where the police at the intersection could see us. I didn't want anyone to break into the car at night since we'd have to leave it here until the evacuation orders were lifted.

Two of Laura's bags were packed full of various supplies. They were heavy and awkward. With Oscar leashed up, we made our way across the street and up Bicentennial. Like yesterday, no one made any move to stop us.

We encountered a few groups of people walking down. These must be other neighbors who had made the trek to check on their houses. By their expressions, I could tell which of them had just discovered that they no longer had a home. There was a seriousness about the people coming down the hill that I normally didn't see in regular day-to-day life. We gave them all a wide berth and walked up the middle of the street.

As we made our way through Miramonte, we saw that the jets of flames from the gas lines had been put out. PG&E, the utility company, must have turned gas off to the neighborhood. Getting rid of those flames was an improvement that made things look marginally less like a hellscape than they had before.

Various news vans with big satellite dishes were parked along the sides of the street, and I saw a news team broadcasting from a burned house. The owner was picking through the rubble, and a journalist was asking him questions. A cameraman stood off to the side, filming the encounter. I couldn't hear what they were saying but could imagine pretty well. I had watched a couple identical interviews on television already.

We wound our way through Miramonte, and then up and around the hill toward Viewpointe. We passed by the back end of the house that Dave and I had talked in front of yesterday. There were ashes and rubble strewn all the way down the hill toward us. I could smell that sulfur-like odor from this side, too, which was something in common with all the destroyed houses we passed.

We walked the rest of the way up the street and came into View-pointe Circle. Wayne was gone, but we saw Dave and waved to him.

"You came back," he said. "Are you staying?"

"Yes," we confirmed, smiling. He seemed happy.

We made our way into our house and let Oscar loose. It was the middle of an evacuation zone, and we had no heat or power, but we were home. It felt good to be back.

We went around and took inventory. Bottled water had been helpful during the earthquake a couple years ago, so we always kept ten gallons or so handy at a time, just in case. I went out to the garage and got one of them. We did have running water, but we had been warned on the news not to drink it, as it was potentially contaminated and unsafe.

While I made my way around and started putting provisions in a pile, Laura added all the new contacts she had acquired to the text thread. By 1 p.m., almost all of the neighbors were on it.

### #VIEWPOINTE STRONG

**LAURA:** If you are receiving this message you have been added to the VIEWPOINTE CIRCLE text message thread

**LAURA:** We are here. Had to walk in. No power.

Although only a few people had seen her post earlier this morning, everyone saw it now. We were officially connected.

**MIKE:** Are they allowing people up?

**RHONDA:** Thank you

**RHONDA:** What is needed? We can bring waters and anything else

Laura and I responded at the same time.

**ME:** They officially are not letting people up.

**LAURA:** They ARE NOT allowing people up here. We parked and walked with our dog. Police report that there have been a few small explosions today.

Propane tanks that hadn't burned in the fire were getting cooked in the smoldering rubble piles and had been exploding one by one. The police at the bottom of the hill by the barricade had heard the pops going on all night long.

**MIKE:** How does our circle look?

**TED:** We're there now! 3 houses gone. Several more with minor damage. You're OK

Ted lived in the house next to the one that had burned down on the corner. Like we had yesterday, he found a way in and was checking things out. When I met him later that day, he credited Dave with saving his house.

Being immediately next to the one that burned down, the radiant heat had blown his windows in, and flames had gotten inside his house. His bed caught fire. Dave, who was a friend and had a key, went inside with Ted's garden hose and managed to put the bed out and keep the fire from spreading.

Later, when I asked Dave for more details, he told me that the heat had been intense. He had only been wearing a T-shirt, which offered no protection, and he almost couldn't stand to be in the bedroom. The hose didn't have a nozzle, and he couldn't find one in time, so he was stuck standing there with only his thumb over the end of it to spray the water. But, as I'd learn over the next few days, Dave can be quite stubborn, so he pushed through and managed to suppress the fire. Ted's bedroom was a disaster, but his house (and probably all the other ones in that row) was still standing thanks to Dave's quick action.

**LAURA:** Going to do recon now. Will text back when done. Turning off cell temporarily to conserve battery.

Laura's was the last post in the thread for a while. The battery issue was a problem. Without power, we weren't able to charge our phones using the wall outlets. We had access to two battery backups from our computers, so we would be able to charge them for as long as they lasted, but options were slim. I wasn't too concerned in the moment because I was expecting to have to hike back down to the car from time to time and go on supply runs. I would be able to charge the phones at that time. We just needed to be careful so that both phones didn't go dead before we had that opportunity.

It was time to look around and get a better feel for the condition of the neighborhood. Oscar also needed a walk. He had been cooped up for too long since the evacuation and was bursting with energy.

We had a special training harness from Oscar's days practicing Shutz-hund, a dog sport that involves obedience, tracking, and protection work. Dogs love it; it's the ultimate form of tug-of-war. Oscar's harness went over his back and around both his front legs. There was a handle on the top where I could grab him if needed but in a way that didn't hurt his neck. We thought it would make him look more official and protective looking if he wore that. We also put his regular pinch collar on as well as his backup flat collar.

Earlier in the year, long before any of the fires had hit, I had taken Oscar out on one of his regular walks. We made it back home, but before we could go in, we had to stop because a young woman walking two white dogs was passing on the sidewalk directly in front of our house. I moved Oscar off the street and told him to "down" on the grass on Elliot's lawn, across the street from our house. He complied, and although alert (as usual), he wasn't growling or causing any issues.

I had seen these dogs many times before, and they always barked and caused a scene whenever they saw another dog. Small dogs are easier to physically control, and people react more favorably to them when they misbehave, since they're cute rather than scary when they're angry, so their owners tend not to spend a lot of time training them or working on their bad habits. These two weren't well behaved at all, which I knew from previous encounters with them. Usually they would bark at Oscar from across the street, and he'd either bark back or would get put in a down, like he was now. On the whole, pretty standard for dog walking in general.

But in this case, something different happened. One of the two dogs looked over at Oscar and barked and growled in a way that was completely challenging and over the top. I don't speak "dog," but even I knew what that little guy said from his tone and expression. He had just cussed Oscar out and insulted his mother.

Oscar reacted immediately. He jumped up in a fury, and I yanked the leash down in response to him breaking his command. He wears a pinch collar, the most common type of collar for working dogs. It gives the owner a lot of control without causing damage or choking the dog. They are formed with a bunch of prongs, connected like links on a chain. As Oscar jumped, one of those prongs suddenly disconnected, and I felt the leash snap off. Oscar was free, and he was pissed off!

He flew into action, sprinting toward those two little dogs. The hair all the way down his back was raised. The white dogs weren't barking anymore, but frozen stiff. Oscar didn't stop running as he got close and took a bite at the one that had caused him trouble as he passed. His momentum carried him through the crowd, and he turned around to make another pass. A tuft of white fur floated in the air. Before he could get fully involved with them, I managed to grab him.

In a dog fight, you don't ever try to grab a dog by the collar. That's a good way to get really hurt. Instead, you get behind them and grab their rear ends, lifting their back legs off the ground like a wheelbarrow. Then you can pull them away without getting accidentally bitten yourself. Some dog breeds, like the Belgian Malinois, have been known to turn on their masters in overly intense situations where they aren't able to get to the other dog, so if you have one of those by the rear end, you can use that position to keep the pointy end away from yourself until the dog calms down.

Once I had Oscar and had angled him away from those two dogs, I was able to get him over to the fence and put him in the backyard. When I came back, the girl was beside herself. At first, she thought Oscar had been running off his leash, but I showed her the leash and how the collar had come apart. She was overwhelmed, and between being mad at me and worried for her dog, she threw up in my yard. Her dogs were actually fine, but I offered to pay the vet bill if she wanted to take them in to be sure. I gave her my phone number, and she left.

Later that day, her father called. I told him the story and reiterated my desire to pay any vet bills that might be required. I answered his questions about Oscar's shots (yes, up to date on all of them), and whether or not he had ever done this before (no, never, which was true). He didn't seem angry with me, just concerned about his daughter.

A week later, I got a call from animal control. The owners of the white dogs had filed a report against Oscar, and he had gotten a strike. One strike is a warning, two means the dog has to wear a muzzle whenever he goes out and a special sign has to be placed in the yard. It didn't matter that there was an equipment failure to blame or that the other dog had started it (right in front of my house), the fact that Oscar was the one that got off the leash made him responsible for the encounter. Oh, and as long as they had me on the phone, they needed me to pay a fee to register Oscar in their database as his registration was for Napa County, not Sonoma. It was a horrible experience.

After that, I vowed never to have a pinch collar failure again. From that time forward, Oscar always goes out with two collars and two leashes. One is the regular leash and pinch, and the other is the backup. I'm not sure what people think when they see me walking a dog with two leashes, but it's my job to keep him safe, and if that's what it's going to take, two leashes it is.

Once we had the dog all geared up, we headed out. First stop was down the tail of the *Q*. There were four houses along one side of the street here, and on the other side was first someone's yard, then additional parking, and then finally a hill that went up to the next street over. The first two houses survived, but the second two were gone. That familiar burnt house smell permeated the area as we stood there, looking over the ruins.

I didn't know who lived at the last house down the Q, but the third one had just been bought by Per and Michelle. Per had been born in Sweden and had given up trying to teach Americans how to pronounce his name properly, so he ended up just telling people to call him "Pear," like the fruit. I first met him at Elliot's "tacky" party two months ago. He hadn't moved in at that point but showed up to meet his new neighbors. I liked Per and had gotten along with him well. I was looking forward to going on bike rides with him once it got warmer. By a strange twist of fate, not only had his new house burned but so had his old one. That had to be tough.

The way the walls had collapsed on Per's house allowed embers to burn protected underneath the rubble. I could see them glowing between the cracks, covered up by big chunks of material that had caved in from the walls and roof. A hose had already been laid out nearby in easy reach by whomever had been working on the embers over the night, and we turned on the water and did our best to soak down what embers we could. The top beam and sides of the garage door frame were still standing, along with the supporting columns, but it all seemed precarious. I was concerned about going too far in and having something crash down on top of me. The big beam across the top in particular looked really heavy. Laura held Oscar, and I picked my way gingerly through some of the initial rubble with the hose to get better angles at the embers, happy to see some of them hiss as the water reached them. There was no way to get all of them, though, and it was clear that this would be an area to keep an eye on in the future.

After we did what we could, we turned around and started our way back from the Q. Despite the fact that Per's house had burned to the foundation, the one next door on the left was fine. Even the fence between them seemed perfect. I couldn't imagine how the heat from Per's fire wasn't able to jump to that fence, which was only a few feet away. None of these houses had much space between them. Fire can be fickle.

As I wondered at that, my eyes drifted to the front door of the house that was standing, and I noticed that it was slightly ajar. *Oh crap.* We froze, the news reports of looters taking advantage of empty neighborhoods fresh on our minds.

Completely alert, I made my way up to the door. The entire frame where the bolt secured the door in place was broken in, the wood splintered and disconnected from the wall. This door had been kicked in from the outside. Whomever had done it knew what they were doing, and I could see a mark just above the door handle where something heavy had been used like a battering ram. The door itself was metal, but the frame was wood, so breaching the door was just a matter of applying enough force to the right spot.

Cautious, the three of us made our way around the back of the house. There were two back doors that led from different rooms to the patio in the backyard. Both of those doors were open. I wasn't about to go wandering through someone's house without a really compelling reason, but I did peek in. The room itself was a mess, with clothes and items thrown haphazardly everywhere. But a TV and some electronics were there and seemed undisturbed. At first, I thought looters had ransacked the place, but on second glance maybe the owners had been in a rush to get valuables out and had engaged in a frantic search in the night. Or maybe they were just messy. It wasn't totally clear. I closed both of the back doors and double-checked the area for spot fires, finding none.

If it had been looters that had gotten into this house, which was my working theory, they had targeted it well. With the two houses next door having burned down, it would have been easy to approach this one without being seen. The hill behind the house provided lots of natural cover, and someone could easily have made their way up the hill from below without anyone else in any of the other houses being any the wiser. It was steep but not impassable, and I myself had wandered around in there last year when I was searching for Squatchie, thinking he was stuck up a tree somewhere. If I were a looter and knew the general lay of the land, that's probably one of the ways I'd have tried to get in, too.

We decided to keep moving and made our way out of the Q and into the larger circle. As you exit onto Viewpointe and turn left, there are two other neighborhoods that you pass on your left before reaching

Fountaingrove Parkway, the route we had taken to evacuate the previous day. Both neighborhoods have roads shaped like a *U*, so that if you drive into them and keep going, you soon find yourself brought right back to Altruria. Viewpointe is the only true circle among the three of them.

Fountainview is the name of the next street up from Viewpointe, and we turned in to explore it. Ten houses had survived, five on the right side of the street and five on the left. The five on the left have backyards that abut those behind the houses on this side of Viewpointe Circle. Fountainview is higher up on the hill, though, so there is a bit of a retaining wall that separates the two neighborhoods' backyards from each other in addition to the fence line. The other five houses on Fountainview were all directly across the street from these.

Things looked fine until we got to the first bend in the *U* on the street, and that's when we realized that these ten houses were all that was left of Fountainview. Everything else had been torched.

We made our way through the middle of the street, taking in the destruction around us. There was glass and debris that blocked sidewalks, and we took care not to let Oscar walk on anything that might cut his paws. All the cars we came across were completely burned out, with only the metal shells and frames remaining. Even the exterior paint had burned off. None had tires, or even wheels. The wheels themselves had melted, and the aluminum had flowed downhill and hardened in strange patterns. Weeks later, I noticed a survivor in a nearby neighborhood had collected some of the patterns and stuck them upright in their yard as a strange kind of decoration.

Now that there were no houses left to block the view, we could see into what had been people's backyards. It made the neighborhood seem a lot smaller than it had before. We noticed a painted ceramic decorative pig in someone's yard that seemed perfectly fine. We both commented on the pig and wondered how that particular item had managed to survive, while everything around it had been turned to ash.

We came upon one car in the road and stopped to investigate further. Like the others, it was just a shell with melted wheels. I noticed that the front windshield had melted and fallen inward, reforming in a strange new pattern around what was left of the dash and front seats. It reminded me of melted cheese. It was impossible to tell anything about what kind of car this had been or how old it was, as all the interior materials were gone. If someone had gotten out of their house late here, they would have perished in the middle of the street, like the cars had. The heat must have been intense. The strangest thing about it was that a lot of mailbox posts seemed totally untouched. Mailboxes and barbeque grills. Aside from that, it was like a bomb had gone off.

We worked our way up the *U* and exited on Altruria, one street higher than where we had entered. We kept going to see how Gardenview, the next street up, had fared.

Gardenview had been hit even harder. There was only one house on the entire street that had survived. Everything else was obliterated. The sulfur smell was strong, and we quietly walked through the area, remarking on the remains of houses that we recognized from previous walks we had taken. Even Oscar seemed to understand that none of this was normal and that we were in the middle of a disaster.

I couldn't help but wonder what was different about that one blue house that helped it to survive when none of the other houses had. It was located in a small cul-de-sac off the middle of the *U*. It didn't seem to have any particular advantage over any of the neighbors in terms of location. Had someone stuck around and fought the flames? I doubted it—the smoke from all the other houses burning would have been overwhelming. For whatever reason, this house had been spared. The more interesting question was whether or not the owners were lucky. Yes, their house made it, but now they had to live in what looked like a war zone. All alone.

If there wasn't anyone home—and it would have been suicidal to stay when the rest of the neighborhood was going up in flames—then that house would be a sitting duck for looters. Might as well throw out a welcome mat and paint a target on the side of it, exposed as it was in the remains of the neighborhood. There is a safety that comes in numbers, and those people would be alone for a long time. Probably years, given how slow things move in California when it comes to construction regulations and general-purpose red tape when trying to get anything done.

Having seen enough, and not wanting to stray too far out of our area, we headed back to Viewpointe. Dave was there to meet us and give us some masks to wear. They were like doctor's masks, which cover your mouth and nose, but had the addition of a particulate filter on the tip, which made them better for smoke.

"This is the best kind," he told us as he handed them over. They were still new in their plastic containers. Some supplies had made their way up the hill, probably delivered by Ted and Cathy, and it was clear that these had been high on Dave's request list.

After we got home, Laura restarted her phone and texted an update to the thread.

## #VIEWPOINTE STRONG

LAURA: 1966, 1934, and 1930 are gone. I'm so sorry. 1962 has minor damage to one side.

HOLLY: 😧thanks for the update

MIKE: Is there any update on when we might be able to get back?

TED: Not yet

Dave's wife Bonnie replied next. She was tech savvy and tended to dictate her replies rather than type them, so her texts were always long and borderline run-on sentences. Dave, on the other hand, was the opposite. Although he had a cell phone, he never used it.

BONNIE: Hi Michael. Dave was told earlier today that it could be several weeks before we have power back. So you can park by any of the fire gates and you could walk in. And we would recommend that anybody that has a refrigerator full of food do so because your refrigerator needs to be emptied and then left propped open otherwise it's going to ruin the refrigerator

**MIKE:** Thank you for the information!

**LAURA:** If anyone can't make it in to clean your fridge, I can try to do it. Please let me know. Laura

**ELLIOT:** We are coming up tomorrow with Gary and maybe Holly to do it

**MIKE:** Jodi and I might be heading up tomorrow or Thursday

**BONNIE:** Hey gang when you do go up there can you guys please check on Dave he is so exhausted. I really hope with Earik and Laura there tonight that he gets some sleep

**MIKE:** Will do!

After what Dave had told me about the dangers of falling asleep and getting burned alive after a hot spot flared up, I had no doubt that he wasn't sleeping much. Now that there were people in the neighborhood to help, he didn't have to try to do everything himself anymore, which must be a huge relief. There were five of us that showed up, intending to spend the night. In addition to Laura and me, there was Sebastian, Eddie, and TJ. This was the first time I'd laid eyes on any of those three. None of them had ever attended any of the potlucks. I hadn't seen Wayne all day and assumed he was working, but I would be surprised if he didn't turn up at some point, too.

Eddie and TJ lived in the same house toward the entrance to the circle. Eddie is a burly Asian guy that works in technology. He has just the faintest hint of gray on the sides of his head. TJ is a young, slightly overweight Latino college student, who I've never seen without his hat. Eddie's girls would visit him every couple weeks, but there was too much space in the house for him alone, so TJ rented the room above the garage. The two of them were close friends despite an age difference, and they had a great sense of humor, always joking around. Laura had added Eddie to #VIEWPOINTE STRONG but was having trouble with TJ since he didn't have an iPhone and Apple wasn't playing nice with adding his number to the group thread. Until those details were worked out, he mostly communicated with the group through Eddie.

**EDDIE:** Hi Neighbors, it's Eddie and TJ. We are in-house and will keep an eye on the hood! Holla if you need anything!

**BONNIE:** Thanks

**ELLIOT:** Keep one eye open tonight for any unwelcome visitors 😶

**ME:** Oscar is going to get so many walks tonight that he'll think he won the lottery 😄

**CARMEN:** You ALL are totally awesome. Thank you for all you are doing. Hugs galore, Carmen and Joe

**BONNIE:** AGREED!

**ELLIOT:** Thank you sooo much

**MIKE:** Thank you! It means a lot to have such great neighbors!

**NICOLE:** So blessed to have you all. Especially Oscar :)

We hadn't organized yet, and none of us had much of a plan, but we were already beginning to come together as a community to protect the neighborhood and each other.

# CHAPTER 5

# Sleeping on the Couch

ON ONE OF my trips to check on the embers down the $Q$, I ran into Joe and Carmen driving up in their red Prius. Somehow, they had managed to get a car past the barricade. Joe slowed and rolled his window down, reaching out to grab a hold of my arm affectionately. Goldie was lying in a flexible cat carrier on Carmen's lap.

"How did you manage to drive up here?" I asked.

Joe told me that he had come in through the fire gate on one of the side streets. It had been wide open, and he drove right through. That was valuable information, and I thought of my SUV still parked down on the other side of the police line.

Evacuating in a car is infinitely preferable than having to do so on foot, especially if there are heavy flames and smoke to deal with, so if there was a way to get my car up here, I was going to try. After saying goodbye to Joe and Carmen, I started to turn around and go back to my house when Eddie and TJ called to me from where they were standing back toward the entrance to the circle.

"Hey, Earik, do you want to go on a walk with us?" Eddie asked. They were heading up toward Fountainview and Gardenview.

"No, I'm actually going to get my car."

Eddie checked his watch. "Don't forget about the curfew!"

In response to issues that they were having with looters and keeping people out of mandatory evacuation areas in general, the director of Santa Rosa Emergency Services had imposed a curfew on all evacuation areas. Anyone found out and about in an evacuation zone between 6:45 p.m. and 7:15 a.m. would be arrested. We had no plans to follow the curfew, as the embers kept burning through the night whether or not a curfew was in force, but getting caught here in the neighborhood where we lived would be much easier to explain than getting caught somewhere else. If I was going to get my car, I had to hurry.

I went inside and wheeled my mountain bike out of the garage and through the living room. I quickly put on my helmet, made sure I had keys, and let Laura know what was happening.

And then I was off, flying down the hill and back through Miramonte. I went fast, and it only took a couple minutes to get down past Home Depot and to the other side of the police line. I dismounted, went to the stoplight, and the traffic cop stopped traffic and let me pass. I thanked him, jumped back on my bike, and rode over to my car.

Usually I throw my bike in the back, but I had forgotten about Oscar's kennel that was still in there. I had a surge of panic as I realized I might not be able to fit my bike in the car. I didn't have rope to tie it to the roof. *Leave the kennel and make two trips?*

In the end, my solution was to stuff the bike in the back seat. I had to push the bike's seat all the way down as low as it would go and take the front wheel off, but I managed to squeeze it all in there. The bike rested at an awkward angle, but with some force I was able to get the doors closed, and that's what counted.

Then I started up and drove away from Bicentennial, heading up the side streets and making my way toward the neighborhood at the south end of Fountaingrove.

I was actually quite familiar with this neighborhood and had taken Oscar on walks here many times. These houses bordered right up against the edge of our area, but there were no roads that actually went through to connect them. There were two fire gates, though.

The first was all the way up Terra Linda, at the very end of the road. There was a big metal gate that swung on a hinge, and it allowed fire trucks to get from here to Lake Park, which is the road that we had used to make our way from Home Depot up to the entrance to Miramonte this morning. It was the most obvious gate to try, as anyone who drove through the area would have known about it. As I got closer, I saw a police cruiser pulled across the back end of the gate, blocking it. *Not that one...!*

I turned around and headed back, working my way up toward Baldwin. The street ended in a cul-de-sac, and there were four wooden poles resting in holes in the ground on one side of it. Without those poles in place, this cul-de-sac would connect directly to another one on the other side. On my walks, I'd usually come through this gate, walk along the streets on this side, and then go home via the other fire gate where the cop had been.

Thankfully, unlike that other gate, there was no police presence here, and although the poles were in their holes, they were not padlocked in as usual. The neighbors here had access to the keys, and someone had unlocked them.

I pulled up and made my way over to look at the poles. The guardian, who was a neighbor off to the right working in her garage, came out when she saw me.

"Do you live here?"

"Yes. I live on Viewpointe Circle."

She studied me for a moment, trying to determine if she should ask further questions, but decided that I was telling the truth. "OK. Just make sure to replace the posts after you go through."

I removed the two center poles, drove through the gap, and then replaced them. From here, I was only a few turns and a hill away from merging onto Altruria, getting me right back to Viewpointe. It was all done in plenty of time to avoid being caught driving around outside of curfew.

It was starting to get dark, and Laura and I decided to take Oscar out on another patrol. Our plan was to make a complete pass of the circle and surrounding areas at least once every couple of hours. That would give us lots of opportunities to catch any spot fires that might flare-up, as well as provide some security for the neighborhood. It wasn't so much an issue about trying to actually catch any looters but more about establishing a presence in the neighborhood. Oscar is good at doing that, and he has no trouble barking and causing a scene if he sees something he doesn't like. It's not a trait that endears him to neighbors in regular times, but these weren't regular times.

We spent a lot of time joking between ourselves about how this was Oscar's moment. "Finally, you guys! I've been waiting seven years for this!" we'd say in our best Oscar voices. From his perspective, things couldn't have been better—he got to work all day long, was encouraged to bark and be protective to his heart's content, and he had a purpose. That's a huge step up from the pet dog role that he usually had to take on, and I could see by the spring in his step that he was loving every moment. He knew he was working.

As we headed out to patrol the back side of the houses down Altruria, we came upon the rest of the neighbors who were staying the night. Wayne had returned and was talking with the gang. He was dressed in a green tactical outfit and looked very official. The others stood in a loose circle around him.

He spotted us and came over to talk. I held back with Oscar, and Wayne and Laura greeted each other, shaking hands. As he made a move to come over to me, I shook my head and pointed at Oscar, who stiffened as he saw a stranger touch Laura.

"Not friendly," I explained. Oscar wasn't always comfortable with people approaching him or his people head-on. I usually just told people not to even try to meet him. It kept things simple.

Wayne paused and then smiled in understanding. "That's how I like them!"

He had brought more supplies to add to the growing pile of

provisions in front of his house and made sure that everyone knew they were welcome to take whatever they needed. He was only stopping by for a short time and had to go back to work. They had him on an insane schedule, as the city was scrambling to deal with the situation.

We told them we were going to patrol, and they all waved and continued socializing. We made our way down the hill, walking toward Miramonte.

Halfway down, we saw a couple riding up on bikes. They stopped, pulled over, and got off to do something in the brush on the other side of the street, leaving their bikes.

Laura made her way over to them and asked, "Is everything OK?" I didn't hear their response but saw her nod and talk a bit. Then she came back.

"They're putting out a fire," she explained. I could see them stomping the ground and kicking dirt.

We continued down, and then stopped and turned around at the base of the hill by the entrance to Miramonte. We crossed over and came back on the other side of the street. When we passed where the couple had been, we saw that they had rolled a log full of embers out onto the sidewalk where it could burn out without catching anything else on fire. I could easily see where they had stomped the rest of it out.

One thing I noticed about nightfall is that it became much easier to spot embers in the dark. They might remain hidden during the day, but they were impossible to miss at night. They were all over Miramonte, scattered almost all the way up the side of the street closer to that neighborhood. A sea of small orange lights. I became concerned as we made our way back toward Viewpointe, as many embers were in areas that were still heavily wooded.

We got back and scrounged for dinner. Power had been out since the evacuation, so we made due with what food we hadn't thrown out in the refrigerator purge earlier. We had a whole stack of pita bread and hummus, plus a lot of fruit and granola bars. Not the kind of thing I'd normally choose to eat for dinner, but not bad either.

Before he and Carmen had left, Joe had stopped and dropped off an electric lantern for us. It was shaped just like the kerosene lanterns that my dad had brought camping when I was little, except instead of using a flame as a light source, it used a special LED bulb. It was powered by eight D-cell batteries, and if set to the most economical setting, it could be left on for ten days straight. The lantern completely illuminated whatever room we were in, and it let us save the batteries in our flashlights. We used it as our primary inside light source the entire time the power was out, and I thought so much of that little lantern that I went out and bought one weeks later so we could have our own for the future.

After dinner, Laura set up a new group text thread, just for the people staying at the circle. It would make things more efficient if we needed to coordinate with each other. It also would keep the stress off the neighbors who had evacuated. It was clear that many of them were better off not knowing the exact details of what was happening, especially since there was nothing they could do to help.

Eddie was the first to make use of the new thread.

## Group Text

9:17 p.m.

**EDDIE:** It's Eddie. Going on a quick patrol around the circle.

**SEBASTIAN:** I'll come down

**LAURA:** We will do our next loop and down Altruria at 10:30

Given the situation outside, and Dave's warning from the previous day, neither one of us thought it was a good idea to sleep upstairs. Instead, we camped out on the sectional sofa, fully dressed. Laura took one end, and I took the other. Oscar slept on his bed in the corner between us. Aside from the big window in front, we had all the shades up. We wanted to be able to see outside as easily as possible.

We also decided to leave Joe's lantern running through the night. I felt that it would be best if it was very obvious that someone was staying here, and nothing would do that better than a light in the house. Looters were looking for empty houses, not occupied ones, so I thought if they saw the light they'd automatically steer clear. I also wanted any police who might come by to know we were here, too. The last thing you want is for a police officer to spot you sneaking around in your own house with a flashlight and mistake you for a looter.

We used the alarms on our phones to tell us when to wake up for our next patrol. That gave us an hour or two of sleep between shifts. It didn't make for a restful night, as by the time I had settled in from the last patrol, it seemed like I had to get up again to do another.

It was cold outside, so we wore jackets and hats when we made our rounds. We'd wear our breathing masks, too, especially when near burn areas, but they were awkward and hard to get around with. Sebastian was probably the best about wearing his regularly. Dave was the worst. I didn't see him wearing a mask once the entire time. Being a heavy smoker, Dave had given up on lung health a long time ago.

Our patrols would take us around the circle and down the tail of the Q, and we'd randomly check the sides of houses and in the backyards to make sure no embers had flared up. Per's house always deserved a bit of a spraying, as it was continuously smoldering. In the beginning, Laura and I would also take Oscar down Altruria toward Miramonte, but things didn't feel nearly as safe on the outside of the circle and we eventually got tired of walking up that hill. As the night wore on, our focus shifted mainly to the circle proper, rather than the surrounding area.

As we were coming home after one patrol, we encountered a police cruiser driving slowly through the neighborhood. Laura was on the inside of the street, and Oscar and I were on the outside along with a couple of the guys that we had met up with on our walk. The police turned their spotlights on us as they pulled up next to Laura to talk.

"Are you OK?" the officer asked her.

"Yes. We're doing circles."

They studied everyone for a moment, getting a feel for the situation. It didn't take long. "Be careful," they told her and then drove off.

There was no comment about the curfew. They knew what we were doing and probably didn't have time to give us trouble anyway, given that we were residents and not looters. Looters most likely didn't bring their dogs along for walks in the neighborhoods they were plundering.

After we had gotten back, we settled into our spots on the couch and tried to get some rest. My body was beginning to feel wobbly; it didn't like getting up so many times in the night.

BOOM!

We were both startled awake by a huge explosion. I quickly sat up and looked out the back window. A giant plume of flame rose into the sky, towering over the hills around it. It must have been over a hundred feet high.

"What was that!?" I could hear the concern in Laura's voice.

Obviously, something big had just blown up. I was trying to figure out where the flames were coming from. My best guess was Home Depot.

"I wonder if some giant propane tank just exploded," I said, trying to understand what I was looking at. The flames were bright orange and growing. I thought they were huge before, but now they were impossibly taller. It was a towering inferno of rage and anger, throwing its malice across the hills toward us as we watched it through the window. The room was bathed in an orange glow.

Aside from the initial shock in seeing this fireball materialize just over the hill, we both got concerned over what it might mean for us. Could that explosion start another fire? Could it make its way over toward Viewpointe?

One thing we had in our favor was that the explosion happened on the other side of Miramonte, which had already burned. There was no more fuel left in that neighborhood, so it provided a kind of buffer. It was also happening closer to 101, right near the police line, and I hoped that meant emergency crews were close at hand. There was nothing for us to do. We watched and waited.

The flames eventually began to subside, and the height of the plume shrank. Either someone was putting it out or it had burned up all of its fuel. The orange turned to a brown, and the light no longer lit up the sky as it had in the beginning. After a few minutes, it shrank back under the hill top, and we could no longer see it. It was hard to sleep after that.

At 1:25 a.m., a text came through from Sebastian.

### Group Text

**SEBASTIAN:** Let me know about the next patrol Eddie

**ME:** I'll go with you if you want

**ME:** It's about time for one now anyway

**SEBASTIAN:** Sounds good, I'll head out

I left Oscar at home and made my way down the street toward Sebastian's house. He lived at the end of the circle opposite the tail of the *Q*, next to Dave.

Sebastian had been on his way out of the country for a trade show and was staying at a hotel on the East Coast when he woke up to find his phone overwhelmed with missed calls and text messages. He told me that there were so many that he actually thought his phone had crashed or that it had picked up some kind of virus. There were just too many messages. Then he started reading them.

Rather than making the trade show, he immediately turned around and booked a last-minute flight back to California, which he barely made. He was able to talk people into letting him cut ahead of them in the security line by showing them pictures of the fire on his phone and explaining what was happening. He had been the first neighbor who returned to stay full time. Dave, having been all alone and under a huge amount of stress, said he wanted to kiss him on the lips when he first saw him.

At first, Sebastian didn't think it was a good idea to stick around, but once he found out that Dave was a retired firefighter and knew what he was doing, he changed his mind. "You just tell me what to do and I'll do it," was his approach. He was young and willing, and Dave had the experience, so the two of them made a good team. They had already done a lot of work before the rest of us returned.

Sebastian and I met and made our way down the Q, checking all the usual spots. When we were behind the house with the kicked-in door, Eddie joined us. We spotted a big ember down the hill past the final house on the Q. It was too difficult to get down there in the dark, so we decided to make sure to deal with that particular ember in the morning. It was right in the middle of the forested area behind the houses, and a fire there could easily make its way up to us. That wasn't a good ember.

We walked along the houses, checking backyards and looking for embers. There had been more smoldering at Joe and Carmen's that we had to contend with, but nothing serious.

When we got to Elaine's house, which was on the other side of mine from the tail of the Q, Laura called. She heard people talking and wanted to make sure that it was us. I could hear Oscar barking at us from inside. I gave her the "all clear," and we made our way into Elaine's backyard.

Elaine is an elderly woman who has always been very welcoming and friendly to us. She lives with Benny, a small white dog, who doesn't have any teeth left. Our cat Peaches has adopted them as his second family. He'll go right into Elaine's house through the dog flap on her back deck and take naps in Benny's bed. Benny sleeps next to him on the floor. Elaine loves it, and it's all very cute, but I sometimes worry that Peaches might be a little too friendly for his own good. Whenever we can't find Peaches, we know that he's probably hanging out with Elaine and Benny.

The three of us made our way onto Elaine's back deck, looking for embers in her yard. I went first, and after a few steps I felt the wood start to crack under my feet.

"Careful!" Sebastian and Eddie warned, preventing me from going any farther.

"That part of the deck is burned," Sebastian said. "You can fall right through if you go out there."

I pulled back, shining my flashlight on the burned-out sections of

Elaine's deck. The fire had gotten really close. It was a miracle Elaine's house was still standing.

We didn't find any embers and continued our way around the circle. I took my mask off, and let it hang loosely around my neck by the fasteners. It was impossible to talk or breathe with. I would put it on when I went near any of the destroyed houses, but otherwise it felt like more trouble than it was worth. Everything smelled like smoke without it, but at least I could breathe. I tried not to think of what the long-term health effects might be from that decision.

The three of us parted ways and agreed to meet up again for another patrol at five in the morning. It was freezing, and I was glad to get inside and under a blanket.

After an hour or two, Laura and I tried to take another walk around the circle, but Oscar vetoed the motion. It was the only time in his life that I've ever seen him not want to go on a walk. His harness was a little tight and had chaffed him in his armpits, which had begun making him uncomfortable. It was also dark, and cold, and probably smelled even worse to him than it did to us. So he refused, and Laura and I left to do a quick lap around the circle ourselves. It was definitely spookier without Oscar, but we didn't encounter anything and went back quickly.

When I heard my alarm for the 5 a.m. patrol, I had trouble getting my body vertical. Taking short naps between patrols was helpful, but it didn't relieve the tiredness that was starting to set in. I dragged myself out from under the blanket and left into the cold to join the others. Laura and Oscar were happy to stay behind and be in charge of guarding the couch.

Eddie and Sebastian were already together down the street when I joined them. Dave opened his door and came out, too. We all said a quick "hello," and went over to investigate the houses closest to the one that had burned out on the corner.

We made our way down along the side of one and up onto the deck. It was clear that Sebastian and Dave had been here before many times and knew where to check for potential embers. There were none to be found, and as we stood there, Dave told us the story of what had happened in the backyards.

"I was out here, standing on this deck, and was watching the fires come up the back of the hill. All the backyards were getting hit, all at the exact same time. I looked down and saw fire below me through the spaces in the boards." He pointed down at the deck we were all standing on to show exactly where he had been.

"When I went down, I saw that the fire was burning the side of the house and was on the verge of getting inside. It was too much for me to deal with alone, and it was happening all along the row. All of these houses were getting ready to go up. If one goes, they all go, and we lose the neighborhood. We were in trouble.

"So I ran out and, by some miracle, found a fire engine parked up the street. It was pure luck that they were there, right when I needed them. I told them what was happening, but they said they didn't have enough people to handle it."

He then paused to explain what that meant, "You see, it would actually take two engines to be able to deal with a fire like this, because there aren't enough lines on just one to cover the area. One wasn't enough.

"But I told them who I was and said 'You need to see this.' I forced the lieutenant to come and pointed out what was happening. When he saw it, he said 'Fuck!,' then ran back to the engine. By another stroke of luck, a second engine was just pulling into the area. That gave them enough lines, and they were able to knock down everything along these backyards. Had they not been there, in that moment, when I most needed them, the neighborhood wouldn't be here. We're very lucky. Someone is looking out for us."

Those must have been the two fire trucks that I saw the previous day, when the firefighters had been sleeping in people's yards. It had been a closer call than I had thought.

The next morning, #VIEWPOINTE STRONG was buzzing with activity. Many neighbors that hadn't been back yet planned to come today to clean out their refrigerators and wanted to know if there was anything they could bring. D batteries and water were high on the list.

At 8:40 a.m., Eddie posted to the thread.

## #VIEWPOINTE STRONG

**EDDIE:** Got some beef stew with rice here.

**EDDIE:** Makes one hardy breakfast.

Bonnie chimed in with a reminder to the team staying in the neighborhood.

**BONNIE:** Remember today as the winds pick up if at any point you feel you need help from professionals up there please text this list right away. Ted and I can start reaching out to everybody and anybody to get fire trucks up there

**LAURA:** That is great! Thank you!

It was a good plan. There were a lot of evacuated neighbors who were sitting and waiting at hotels with a lot of time on their hands. If the forward team ran into trouble, they would be the perfect resource to rely on to try to get help. We would soon take them up on their offer.

Laura and I decided to make a trip out to take showers at Judith's. We had left some luggage and a lot of other items, like medicine and computers, over at her house, and we wanted to move a lot of that home now that we were back. It seemed like a better idea to keep our most valuable things close by, rather than cluttering up Judith's house with them. We also both had a craving for lattes and bagels at our favorite coffee shop in town.

Before we left, we made our way over to Eddie and TJ's house, which had become a sort of meeting spot for the group. Eddie had the garage open, and a few chairs were arranged inside for people to sit and chat. We told the gang that we were going to head out for an hour and got a Starbucks order together for them. As long as we were going out, we were definitely going to try to bring goodies back to the neighborhood.

We moved Oscar's kennel inside and got him situated.

## #VIEWPOINTE STRONG

**LAURA:** Our dog is in a crate in the living room and key is under welcome mat. We are heading out for showers. If there is a fire while we are gone, please save Oscar!!

We headed out, winding down the streets to arrive at the Baldwin gate with the four poles. As before, I removed a couple, made my way through, and then replaced them.

Eddie texted the thread, concerned about his rapidly diminishing battery power.

**EDDIE:** Wayne, where did you get the battery cell with the USB ports? I understand that this device is good to charge phones?

**WAYNE:** That battery is located inside the ice chest in front of my house help yourself

**ME:** Laura and I are bringing up a portable car jumper that can also charge USB devices. We'll have it when we get back

We had been charging our phones using the two backup batteries for our computers. Once the power went out, they'd kick in to provide full power for a period of time but would beep continuously while doing so. We moved them into the closet downstairs and charged our phones with the door closed so that the beeping would be less annoying. Laura's unit had already died, and mine wasn't far behind.

**EDDIE:** Thanks team!

**EDDIE:** Looks like the battery cell is checked out. Masks would be helpful.

**WAYNE:** COPY

**WAYNE:** If anybody can stock my ice chest and put soda in, it will help with keeping the professionals to hang around as they take short breaks. Snacks too

Wayne had done his best to stock the refreshment center in front of his house, but as long as people were asking how they could help, it made sense to get them involved. Not only would it be helpful to any police or firefighters that might need it, the rest of us at the circle could use some supplies as well. Yesterday we had all scrounged for our meals.

Laura and I made it to the coffee shop on our way out and noticed how many first responders were there this morning. Coffee was free to any first responder who wanted it, and by the looks of things, there were a lot of them who needed it! As I waited for my bagel, I studied the uniforms of all the different people that came in, noting what city they came from. There were teams in from all over the Bay Area and even farther out. Emergency crews were really chipping in to help deal with the fire. Santa Rosa was not alone.

Shortly after coffee, as we got close to Judith's, a disturbing text came through.

**EDDIE:** Guys hold off on coming up the police are here and encouraging us to leave. Stand by

I didn't like seeing that. Oscar was locked in his cage, and we weren't nearby. I didn't want him to get stranded if the police locked down the neighborhood while we were gone. Laura didn't like it either, so we didn't linger at Judith's. We got our supplies, packed the car, and left. Judith was worried for Oscar, too.

As we made our way back, another update came through.

**EDDIE:** Per Bonnie/Dave we are being told that the city is calling in the national guard to enforce evacuation areas.

*Oh crap!* We had made a mistake leaving Oscar. I wasn't sure how he would react if someone came to get him out of our house accompanied by the national guard. I could think of a lot of ways that scenario might play out in ways that weren't pretty. I was even more concerned that Oscar might get left behind, locked in his kennel in an evacuated neighborhood with no way for us to get to him. I had a vision of myself dressed in black, sneaking through backyards in the night to try to break into my own house to rescue my dog. I tried not to think about it and sped up. The Starbucks run for the gang wasn't going to happen.

**LAURA:** We are on our way back.

We got another concerning text immediately after that.

**BONNIE:** hey everybody heads up please get on your phones begin calling emergency numbers begin calling anybody pulling any strings you can to get a fire truck up there because 1934 is smoldering badly Dave is concerned please spread the word

That was Per's house. It had been smoldering since I had first seen it. Something must have happened to make it worse if Bonnie was putting the call out like that. Had it burst into open flame again? Now my fear was not that Oscar would be left alone, but that the neighborhood might go up and he'd be burned alive, trapped in his cage without a way out. I was kicking myself as we flew back home, pedal on the gas. *Drive fast, just don't get pulled over!*

**BONNIE:** We're going to start calling the non-emergency numbers and the radio stations to see if we can't get some-body up here for 1934

**WAYNE:** Trying to pull strings but they have designated our area as a "burn area" and no resources will be sent I'm told.

Bonnie posted a phone number to the text thread.

**BONNIE:** Please start calling this number it's the emergency services coordination line. I begged her I said that there were a few people up there that people were getting ready to leave and that there were over 34 homes that are still standing and I started crying and please do whatever you can guys

To add to the anxiety, Wayne texted.

**WAYNE:** Nicole if you are monitoring this thread call me NOW!!!

**WAYNE:** Nicole please ASAP!!!

Nicole is Wayne's wife. I had no idea what was going on. This is not the kind of conversation I wanted to see happening right as soon as I had left the neighborhood. The thread went deathly silent for almost ten minutes. Laura held her phone in her hand as we drove, zipping in and out of traffic, trying to get home as fast as we could.

**NICOLE:** Talked to Wayne.

*And… ? Come on, Nicole!* I never found out what it was about but hoped that whatever it was wasn't news that Viewpointe was gone, along with Oscar and everyone else.

Bonnie texted some good news after this.

**BONNIE:** Hey everybody we may have just had a miracle Sheri from the circle above us called the number and she got patched through to an actual fire chief and he said he was going to send trucks up there as soon as possible please pray it's true pray he follows through it's a number we were not supposed to have

A few minutes later, Eddie confirmed.

**EDDIE:** Fire Marshall is here

That was good news! Laura and I had made it back toward Baldwin, and I was relieved to see the gate was still unguarded. It was open, and we cruised in. Once through the poles, I knew we'd be able to get back to Oscar and felt relieved.

**LAURA:** We're in

**EDDIE:** Good

When we returned, we found that two fire trucks had pulled into the circle. I parked in our driveway and went out to see what was going on. One crew was investigating the houses down the *Q,* while the other checked out the burned house on the corner. I went over to that one and watched as they looked around and talked among themselves. A third engine eventually showed up as well.

After a short period of time, they all loaded up and left. None of the firefighters made eye contact as they drove away. They had decided not to do anything. There were more pressing needs than soaking down houses that had already burned in an area that was a mandatory evacuation zone. Their primary concern was saving lives, not houses. Property would always come second behind lives, and not everyone was safe yet. They made a loop around the circle and were gone.

**EDDIE:** Cal fire says we are on our own. Our area is not a priority

Wayne clarified.

**WAYNE:** Hey "not a priority" are my words these guys are doing what they can just keep that in mind and don't panic...

**TED:** Ok—not panicking

**LAURA:** lol. This is me calm.

We tried to take it in stride. We understood their logic, and we knew we'd probably make the same decisions if we were in their shoes. But in our hearts, watching them leave, we couldn't help but feel abandoned. Three houses had burned, and one threatened to take down all the others. We could see the smoke and feel the warmth. The fire was there with us in the neighborhood. Lurking, threatening. Almost like a looter scoping out its next target, but one without any care for self-concealment. And the people who could stop it just told us we weren't important enough to waste any time on.

It was up to us. We were the fire department now. Since they didn't want to deal with Per's smoldering house, we handled it ourselves the best way we knew how. We found someone's oscillating lawn sprinkler—the kind that sits in one place and sprays water back and forth—and put it out right in the middle of Per's rubble pile. We ran a really long hose over from his neighbor's house and let it crank, moving it around to adjust the position from time to time. The next month, the neighbor whose water we used posted their 9000-gallon water bill to the thread, and it was not pretty. But in the moment, drenching Per's house was a top priority, and we sure drenched it. That sprinkler ran for days.

# CHAPTER 6

# Pointe Patrol

A LOT OF people had made their way back to Viewpointe; the neighborhood was humming with activity. Elliot, from across the street, and Mike, who lived next door to him, were both actively out and about, helping with various tasks and checking in on everyone who had stayed. Others came and went all morning.

The main job was emptying refrigerators and leaving them propped open to avoid mold growth. This was the third day since the evacuation, and food had already started to rot.

The house next to the entrance to the Q had an issue. During the wind storm the night of the evacuation, a large tree branch crashed down on the back of the BMW in their driveway. The rear window was completely shattered, and the driveway was blocked with debris. Luckily, this had all happened after these neighbors had already evacuated. A number of people helped to drag the branches off the car, stacking them in a pile on the sidewalk.

Strangely, within minutes of having cleaned that tree branch away, we all heard a loud cracking sound and another one came crashing down in the front yard of the house next to Eddie's. It missed his car by only a couple feet. Luckily no one had been standing there when it happened, as it was a highly trafficked area.

We all looked at each other with relief after realizing what had happened. It was a close call. We stacked those branches as well to get them out of the way.

Laura and I had three fold-out plastic picnic tables and twelve chairs in our garage. Laura uses them for various groups that she facilitates on the weekends. As Eddie's house had become the main meeting point, we needed more than a couple chairs for people to sit on, so TJ helped me carry all of our supplies over. Someone went over to Agnes's place, where the tree branch had just fallen, and moved her big umbrella out to the front by the tables for shade. A few more of us hauled Eddie's big barbeque grill out to the front so we'd have a place to cook by the tables. It made Eddie's driveway much more inviting than it had been, and now people could come and take breaks and visit with each other when they weren't working.

This meeting point soon became crucial to the community and became our de facto headquarters. We met here, ate here, relaxed here, and guarded the entrance from here. It was our nerve center.

Since it was no longer just Eddie and TJ's driveway, but something much bigger and more important, we discussed various names for what to call it. "Fireside Café" was a funny suggestion and one of my favorites, but in the end, we settled on "Viewpointe Café."

One of Wayne's buddies from work showed up in a pickup and unloaded two small chainsaws from the back. He fired one up and began cutting up the two branch piles that we had arranged. As he cut them down to manageable pieces, people jumped in to stack them and get them out of the way. The visiting neighbors took this opportunity to be helpful, knowing that the rest of us were beat after staying up without a lot of sleep. It didn't take long before the branches were cleaned up and no longer a hazard to anyone passing by in the night.

When he was done, Wayne's buddy told Laura and me about the

phone call he had received from Wayne earlier that day. Wayne stood by, listening with a grin.

"I've known this guy for years, and he's as cool as they come. I've seen him in the craziest, messiest situations, and he's always totally calm..." He changed his voice to mimic Wayne speaking, holding an imaginary phone up to his ear. "I need you to come in here with the truck, and then the rest of you work your way around the back side... ," he said, pretending to be Wayne giving instructions in the middle of some deadly standoff. It was clear both he and Wayne had worked SWAT together at some point.

"But today, I get a phone call from him, and he's like 'Fuck! Do you have chainsaws? I need fucking chainsaws! Get me some fucking chainsaws! I need them now! I need them *yesterday!*'" He had dropped back into mimicking Wayne's voice, talking really fast.

"I told him, 'Wayne. Slow down, buddy. Take a deep breath. Now start from the beginning...'" Wayne was laughing to himself as he was being made fun of.

His partner continued, "I saw a doctor—with my own eyes!—who cut open a seven-year-old right along the chest and reached inside to pump his heart with his hand." He reached up, squeezing the air, pumping an invisible heart with his hand. "The doc was just looking at us and chatting, totally calm, as he saved this kid's life. But something happens to his own kid, and the guy's a mess. Totally useless." We all nodded in understanding.

"This was personal," I said, in reference to Wayne's request for chainsaws.

"Yeah," Wayne's buddy agreed. "It was personal." He turned to Wayne, gesturing back with his thumb. "That's your house right there. That's where your kid sleeps at night."

While I had been out and about trying to help out with physical jobs, Laura had been busy trying to organize the group. She had gotten everyone on board for a midday meeting.

## #VIEWPOINTE STRONG

**LAURA:** If you are here, meet in front of Wayne's in 5 minutes to review strategy for tonight

**TED:** I hope Oscar is at the meeting!!!

**LAURA:** Will someone grab Dave. Not sure if his cell is on.

**BONNIE:** Dave is afraid of losing his cell phone while he's fighting a fire. He doesn't always have it on him. So you may have to physically grab him.

We all gathered on Gary's lawn, across the street from Wayne's house. At least half the neighborhood was present, since so many people had come up for the day to clean out their refrigerators and deal with their houses. Dave was the last to join us, walking over from where he had been at his house. We had been waiting for him.

"Hello, everyone," he said in his deep voice as he began his address to us. He wore his large black T-shirt from yesterday. It was a good color choice, given how much soot Dave was still covered in.

"We've been very lucky, and our neighborhood is still here. But this isn't over yet. The forecast is for the winds to pick up tonight, and if that happens, any one of these hot spots could flare-up and we could lose the hood. If we can make it through tonight, there's a good chance we'll be OK. Tonight is critical.

"I'm not your boss. You don't have to do what I say. I'm a neighbor, just like you, trying to save our neighborhood. But I've got some experience, and I'll tell you what I think would be a good strategy.

"A lot of people imagine that fire comes at you quickly, in a wall of flame. That's how they show it in the movies. But this is the urban interface. It's not going to happen like that here. It will develop slowly, and we will have some time to react. We just need to be alert and prepared.

"First of all, how many people are going to stay tonight?"

Those of us planning to stay raised our hands. There were eight of us at the meeting, and one more who joined later. The other neighbors planned to leave after the day's work had been done, before the curfew kicked in.

"What we need to do is break up into teams. Each of our teams will patrol a specific area. Eddie and TJ, you guys take the tail of the Q. Watch that entire area. Sebastian and I will take the back fence line around the edge. Gary, you and Laura can watch the houses between here and Fountainview, as well as the inner circle. Earik, you and Wayne can go up to Fountainview and protect those houses."

Eventually, Wayne ended up floating between groups, as Mike from Fountainview would show up and take his spot as my partner. But we didn't know about Mike, as he hadn't made his way home yet.

"We need to be ready, so that we can react quickly to whatever fire we might find. That means prepping every house. Find the hoses and lay them out either in the street or in the backyard. Test them and make sure someone can get to them quickly. Make sure we've got nozzles on all of them, and that we can just grab a hose and get to work without having to unwind it first.

"Also, we might lose water pressure. If you have a shovel, put it out in your front yard. We may need to use them, and they need to be handy.

"You need to be wearing long sleeves and sturdy boots. A hat to protect your head is a good idea. You may be facing heat and sparks, and you need to protect yourself. Find yourself a pair of work gloves, and make sure to bring your masks."

Gary, whose lawn we were sitting on now, chimed in. "I've got lots of shovels and gloves if people need them. Just let me know." Gary works as a distributor for a hardware store supplier. He had a ton of equipment stashed in his garage and already helped set up the café with coolers and other supplies. He was a very handy guy to have present at a time like this.

Dave continued. "If you have a fire extinguisher, bring it out. Let's put them all at the side of Wayne's house, just inside the gate so that looters don't steal them. Take the safeties off. If there's action in the night, you just want to be able to grab it and use it. You don't want to have to find the safety.

"Take any propane tanks and move them inside the circle. That's the safest place for them. We don't want those to get in the fire." That was good advice. I remembered the propane tank fireball I had witnessed the previous night.

"If you find a fire, and you can't deal with it, call for help. Or call 911. And if it is too much, and it's going to get out of control, then you can tell us to evacuate the neighborhood. But make sure that you really can't deal with it before you tell us to evacuate.

"We're going to try to save the hood, but we might not be able to. If we can't, then we have to evacuate. That means one house. If one house goes, we leave. We aren't going to be able to deal with that with the equipment we have.

"So when you evacuate, you need to alert the rest of us. That means getting in your car and driving twice around the circle with your horn down. I don't mean beeping. I mean you hold your horn completely down and drive twice around the circle."

Dave made sure that we understood the signal. "Anyone can call for an evacuation. When you hear that signal, you stop what you are doing, you get in your car, and you leave. It means that we've lost the neighborhood. You don't have to go far. You can just go down the hill a little ways and watch, but you need to get out. Get your car ready, and make sure it is backed into your driveway and pointed out. You need to be able to jump in and go."

Dave paused. "OK... We need to talk about the people who aren't present. There are two neighbors who are here but aren't part of this effort and don't want to help."

Of course, Dave was talking about Mr. Difficult and his wife. I'm not going to use names, because I don't know their story. In fact, I've never even spoken with this guy despite living in Viewpointe Circle for an entire year. I call him Mr. Difficult because of all the trouble he has caused his other neighbors, many of whom told me their various stories over the next few weeks. He's been in legal battles with them, he's had restraining orders placed upon him by them, and he's driven so fast and dangerously that he almost broadsided Wayne. The neighbors all the way down through Miramonte were upset about how recklessly he drove through the streets. All in all, he was a person that was continuously in conflict with others and who made life difficult for almost everyone else around him. I could have called him many other things besides the relatively tame "Mr. Difficult," which would have probably been more accurate in representing what I heard from others when they discussed his behavior. Pick a more fitting D-word for him if you prefer. Douche-bag, dumbass, and dickhead all work. There are many options.

Mr. Difficult had been here the entire time. I don't believe he had ever evacuated like the rest of us. He hunkered down like a troll under a bridge and guarded his house.

That first day, Dave had gone into Ted's house with the garden hose to try to put out the fire in Ted's bedroom. Before he went in, he stopped and asked Mr. Difficult for help. Mr. Difficult is a young guy, very fit and strong. Dave is old and retired. When the water pressure had dropped, Dave had gone to his own hot tub and filled up buckets, which he carried to throw on the flames. But to keep from getting exhausted, he was only able to fill those buckets up halfway. He needed help. What he needed was Mr. Difficult's muscle.

If this were a feel-good Hollywood story, Dave would have gone to Mr. Difficult and had a heart-to-heart with him. "Yes, we've had our differences," Dave would have said, "but the neighborhood is in trouble, and I need your help. Can you put aside our past issues and be a hero? Will you help me save the neighborhood, Mr. Difficult?" And Mr. Difficult would have buried the hatchet and agreed, and together they would be heroes. The neighborhood would have rallied around them, and they would have become friends for life. Mr. Difficult would have been redeemed, and he'd have found himself overwhelmed with the love and appreciation of neighbors who had once despised him.

But this isn't a feel-good Hollywood story, at least in terms of Mr. Difficult's role in what happened. He flatly refused to help. He was asked to help save a neighbor's house from burning down, and he said "No." Brave enough to stay but not brave enough to work with neighbors that he had past issues with? I still can't get my mind around it. I can't think of a better time to step up than when a neighbor's house is literally on fire and someone comes over to beg for your help. To make it worse, at some point, I'm not sure when, I know he said "Let it burn! Let it all burn!"

And so, despite not technically being alone, Dave had been alone during that critical first day, and had been forced to try to save the neighborhood without help. To his credit, Dave did tell me that at some point Mr. Difficult did apologize for his poor behavior in the past, and in my mind, he gets points for being able to do that. But then, within hours of his apology, he told his wife that Dave was actually starting fires, and the two of them went running out of their house with their phones to record as Dave struggled with trying to put out the fires surrounding the house in the corner that had burned down. Maybe it was mental illness, or maybe he was intoxicated, or maybe there's some other explanation that I simply don't understand. Whatever his reasons might have been, none of it sat well with the neighborhood.

Dave continued with his speech to us, "They're not helping, and they aren't going to know what is going on out here, but if the neighborhood goes up, we don't want them to die. Go to their door, pound on it as hard as you can, and yell 'Fire! Fire! Fire!' They might not open it, but try to warn them anyway."

And that was the end of Mr. Difficult's part in the effort to save Viewpointe, because there is really nothing left to say. He was here most of the time but kept to himself, locked in his house in the dark with all the shades drawn. At some point, when no one was looking, he and his wife left, and then possibly came back. No one really knew. Aside from a bunch of neon glow sticks that he had scattered around his yard, you'd never know there was someone in that house.

Elliot, who was sitting in the grass behind me, took the moment to add some hope to the conversation. "We've come this far, and our neighborhood is still here. I don't think God meant to save us this long, only to let us burn tonight. I think we've been saved because of the people here. Because we care about each other, and we try to do the right thing. This is a special neighborhood. Remember that."

"Thanks, Elliot," Laura said.

After a moment, Dave asked, "Does anyone have any questions?"

I had one. I turned my attention to Wayne, who had been standing to the left of Dave this whole time.

"If we have a gun, should we wear it?"

Wayne seemed a little surprised at first, and it took him a second to reply. He seemed to be running through the pros and cons in his head, looking at me as he weighed the options. After all, California has strict laws about carrying firearms, and open carry is not on the menu during regular times. But this was a special situation.

Wayne pointed a finger at me and said, "Yes!"

So be it. I was going to go home and arm myself. There were too many reports of looters, and Wayne wasn't going to be here all the time. There had been police patrols through the neighborhood but not often enough to be able to count on them in an emergency. We were mostly on our own, and the neighborhood needed protection.

It's not that we were only responding to stories of looters either. Looters had actually come into the neighborhood. Sebastian and Dave had been the first to encounter them. Sebastian had been making his rounds early on and passed by Ted's house. He noticed that the side door, which leads to Ted's wine cellar, was open, and distinctly remembered it being closed earlier. Someone was in there.

He called Dave and asked if he wanted to help check it out. Dave agreed, and the two of them made their way over to Ted's, armed with a shovel. They tried to sound like police and called down authoritatively into the cellar. As they made their way in, they saw two men run around the back and head down Altruria and into another area, eventually driving away in a truck. They were both wearing masks and had clearly been up to no good.

After the fact, Sebastian reported their description to some police officers. "Medium build, blue jeans, a dark sweatshirt, drove a white truck," Sebastian said, rattling off what he remembered of the looters.

Later on, he told me jokingly, "Wait a minute...

"Medium build? I'm medium build...

"Blue jeans? I have blue jeans...

"Dark sweatshirt!? I'm wearing a dark sweatshirt...!

"White pickup truck!? I drive a white pickup truck...!

"I just described me!"

From that point on, Sebastian always wore an orange reflective vest, like the ones on crosswalk guards. He never went out without that vest over whatever he was wearing. He wanted it to be very obvious that he was not trying to hide or look anything like a looter. He was, after all, spending his days and nights snooping around people's backyards all throughout the neighborhood, just like the looters had been. The obvious difference was that he was looking for embers to put out, not for things to steal. But the police wouldn't know that. At least not right away.

This was the official formation of the "Pointe Patrol," as we began to call ourselves. The Pointe Patrol had been operating this whole time but in an unorganized way. Now we were organized. People had jobs and partners, and lines of communication had opened up where there had been none. We didn't call ourselves Pointe Patrol right away—it happened organically on the #VIEWPOINTE STRONG thread. But within a day, that's what everyone used when they needed to refer to us. It is also what we named the smaller text thread, the action thread for the people who stayed.

After our meeting broke up, we all left to attend to different jobs in our various zones. I got a pair of work gloves from Gary's stores and went home to get two or three fire extinguishers, which I dropped off at the side of Wayne's house along with everyone else's. There were a dozen fire extinguishers there, of all shapes and sizes.

I moved our shovel to the front yard, flipping it over so I wouldn't accidentally step on the end in the dark and knock myself out with the handle like in a cartoon. The two propane tanks we had were already out near the sidewalk, a task I had done earlier in the day. After I was satisfied, I armed myself with my revolver, running my belt through the loop on the holster and positioning it by my right hip.

When I came back out, a news crew had pulled into the circle, and a reporter was interviewing Eddie. The cameraman filmed from a short distance away. A lot of neighbors were standing around and watching. I don't watch a lot of news on TV, so I didn't recognize who the reporter was, but everyone else seemed to.

I wasn't sure if it would be a good idea for the news crew to see the gun at my side, so I tied my sweatshirt around my waist and tried to act like there wasn't a bulge there. I didn't want to be broadcasted across the Bay Area and cast as a vigilante up on Fountaingrove, even though that's sort of what we were. Vigilante firefighters, at least.

I moved up next to Elliot and pointed down at my side. "I'm packing," I told him quietly.

He smiled and laughed. "I tried to give a gun to a couple people here, but I couldn't find any takers."

I was surprised at that comment. Guns had always been part of my family, and my dad had taught me how to shoot and be safe around them from a young age.

Speaking of my family and guns, the first white baby born in what was eventually to become the state of Tennessee was a Bean, a distant relative of mine. The Beans were Scots, originally from clan MacBain, and were doubly famous for hitting the liquor way too hard and for their tendency to go berserk with blood rage in battle. It was a small clan compared to others, but a notable one with a lot of stories.

When the Beans came to America and settled in Tennessee in the 1700s, they found themselves in a dangerous territory surrounded by hostile Cherokee Indians. I actually have some Cherokee blood, which tells you that relations didn't remain hostile for long! The Beans made a name for themselves as gunsmiths, and the Bean long rifle was highly sought after in its time. It is valuable as a collector's item today, although no examples have made their way down my particular branch of the family tree. So I come from a long line of gun-loving rednecks.

After Laura and I got married, as we were driving through Vermont on vacation, we had a big argument about guns. She was anti-gun, thought they were dangerous, and didn't want one anywhere in the house. I, on the other hand, had owned .22 rifles since I was a teenager and couldn't understand why she was so strongly against them.

I tried to convince her with different arguments. "In this relationship, I'm the man, and it's my duty to protect the family. That means protecting you and any kids that we might have in the future. A gun is the best way I know to do that. It's part of my job as your husband." That's the cave man argument. I could see that although she got my point, she wasn't totally convinced by it. No one had ever had guns in her family. Her history was different than mine.

"Guns are for more than shooting people. What happens if a wounded animal shows up in your backyard and it's going to die? If you have a gun, you can have compassion and put it out of its misery. Otherwise it might waste away in pain for days." This argument helped a lot. She was an animal lover and always blessed any roadkill that we drove by on the highways, holding up her hand as we passed. That habit had been very endearing to me when I first met her. I worked on her enough and she eventually gave in. Years later, I ended up teaching her to shoot, and she practiced on a collection of old soda cans out in the woods with one of my old .22s.

Although it certainly wasn't likely that a mortally wounded deer would ever show up in our backyard in the city here in Santa Rosa, that wasn't always the case. All sorts of animals had come through our yard in Colorado, and when we lived in Tennessee and North Carolina on acreage, animal encounters were even more common.

I am not a gun nut by any stretch of the imagination, but having one around makes a lot of sense to me. Not only for dealing with wounded or aggressive animals, but in case of once-in-a-lifetime emergency situations. Like if there was a crazy person trying to break into the house.

Or if there were riots happening. Or if space aliens invaded Earth and humanity needed to make a last stand.

Those are all unlikely scenarios but not impossible. Except for the last one maybe! I've personally known a family who had to barricade themselves in against their daughter's enraged ex-boyfriend who was drunk and actively trying to break into the house to do her harm. And riots have exploded in the blink of an eye, triggered by news events. These things happen. Life can be crazy.

In our case, all the neighborhoods around us had been destroyed by fire, and there weren't enough police officers to keep looters from running through them seemingly unchecked. No one would ever have guessed that we'd be in this situation, but here we were. Since I planned ahead and owned a gun, I had the luxury of being able to decide if this situation actually warranted me making use of those Second Amendment rights. I had decided that it did.

It wasn't about actually using my gun or trying to capture any looters. In fact, I had no intention of shooting anyone, even if I did catch them stealing my stuff. The purpose was more to set a boundary. Looters show up because they sense easy pickings. They think no one is home in the entire neighborhood, and that makes breaking in much easier than it would be otherwise. But if a looter sees that there are people around, it interferes with their plans. Things get a lot harder with people around, because now they have to become burglars rather than just looters, and that's a more difficult job. It's easier to get caught. If the people in the neighborhood are armed on top of it all, the situation gets even sketchier for them. There were plenty of other neighborhoods for looters besides ours. The sight of a guy wearing a gun might be all that it took to convince them to move along for lower-risk opportunities. Like having Oscar being visible and doing his patrols, or leaving the lights on all night, it was another way of marking our territory.

# CHAPTER 7

# Getting Ready

AS WE ALL went about doing various jobs, Joe and Carmen texted to the thread. They had taken it upon themselves to do a supply run and get anything that Pointe Patrol might need in the night.

### #VIEWPOINTE STRONG

> **CARMEN:** We are on our way to Friedman's for nozzles. How many if they have them? And they are for home hoses I assume?
>
> **WAYNE:** Yes home nozzles maybe 5 or 6

Within ten minutes, Joe and Carmen had found the nozzles and given us an update.

> **CARMEN:** C&J here. We have nozzles and a generator. Now on an ice search. Hope we can get it all up to those who need it.

Wow, a generator! That would be nice.

Bonnie texted next:

**BONNIE:** Hi Carmen and Joe, Michael just got to his house on Fountainview Circle—he is up there too so you might want to reach out to him as an extra body.

She then posted his cell phone to the thread. Mike lived in one of the surviving houses on Fountainview. Since there was another Mike in the neighborhood, who lived next to Elliot, this new Mike became known in the threads as "Fountainview Mike." He became the ninth member of Pointe Patrol and replaced Wayne as my partner in the zone above Viewpointe.

As all of this was going on, Wayne and I jumped into his car, and he drove us up to Fountainview. It was time to prep this neighborhood for the stand that we might have to make tonight when the winds picked up.

Wayne was really worried about the weather and didn't have an optimistic outlook. "If the winds pick up like they say, we're going to be screwed," he said, listening to a report on the radio.

We split the street between us, Wayne starting on one end, and me starting on the other. The plan was to open all the gates to the backyards and get the hoses tested and arranged for quick use in the night. We didn't know if anyone was home or not, and since we were both armed, we didn't want anyone to freak out and think they were being looted. So we knocked on doors before we did anything, just in case.

Joe texted as we started:

**JOE:** We got ice!!

**LAURA:** Get over here Joe!!

There was no one home in the first house. I found the hose in the front, made sure it worked, and stretched it out all the way to the street. I made sure that there was nothing for it to catch on if someone needed to grab it and run one direction or the other. Then, I made my way around back, opening the gate and leaving it swinging for easy access in the night. The back hose was treated in a similar fashion, except I strung it out and hung the end over the back fence, pointing down toward the house below on Viewpointe. From here, I could look down on the backyard and roof of that house. If for whatever reason there was a fire down there, this would be a good vantage point to launch water onto it.

I made my way out and saw Wayne down the street, dragging hoses around and pounding on doors. His movements were swift and energetic. Two Santa Rosa city employees were parked just across from Wayne. I'm not sure what their official capacity was. They looked like they were surveying damage, but they had come across a hot spot in someone's front yard and were stomping it out and spraying it with a hose. Those hot spots were everywhere.

I moved to the next house and knocked on the door. I thought I saw some motion inside and stepped back so I wouldn't crowd the door and scare the person on the inside. An elderly Asian man opened it cautiously, his wife close behind him.

"Hi," I said. "I'm not a looter." I figured I'd get that part out right away. "I live down below you on Viewpointe Circle. A bunch of us have been working through the night putting out fires, and we're getting the neighborhoods ready for tonight. I'm going around and getting everyone's hoses set up in case there's fire." I then answered the few questions they had and asked permission to go into their backyard, which they granted. They had just come up for a few valuables and were planning to head out in the next few minutes.

I arranged their house as I had the other one, uncoiling all of their hoses and stretching them out straight, making access easy for whomever might need to get to a hose quickly. Any hoses in the backyard were always hung on the fence toward Viewpointe. I tried to keep things as standardized between houses as possible, since it would be the early hours of the morning when any action would be taking place, and it might be hard to see. It was also highly likely the person coming into these yards would be me, as this was my zone, so I made mental notes of everything.

As I mentioned earlier, Fountainview is arranged in the shape of a *U*. There were ten houses that had survived the fire there. Five of them were in a row along the Viewpointe side, taking up one leg of the first part of the *U*. The other five were arranged a little differently. There were three in a row on the street across from the row of five, and then the fourth and fifth were sort of behind those three. The fourth one was the house after the *U* made its first bend, so its driveway was at right angles to the others. Then there was a long driveway next to that fourth house which ran back to the fifth. The fifth house was actually behind the very first two in the row of three. So on that side of the street, it was like a little cluster of houses, rather than a row. I actually think that extended driveway had a lot to do with the fire stopping where it had, as it gave an extra bit of a buffer zone that the fire had not been able to jump over the first night.

Wayne and I finished prepping the houses nearest to Viewpointe, then did the three across from them. The last houses we touched were the fourth and fifth, behind the row of three. These two houses were closest to the destruction, and we encountered another hot spot where the two city employees had been working. We had to stop and drench a lot of the front yard of that fourth house, especially the areas where there were mulch and wood chips. We could see thin wisps of smoke drifting up from the danger areas.

When we got to the last house, we found that they had the front hose tightly coiled in a decorative clay container. The hose was stuck and wouldn't easily come loose from that pot. Rather than spending time fooling around with it, Wayne kicked into the clay with his boot, smashing the pot and freeing the hose. I recognized the same impulse in myself from days ago when I had been struggling to put Laura's fancy computer box together in the dark.

We made our way around back and arranged two more hoses. When we got all the way around the other side, toward the burn area directly behind the house, Wayne discovered a huge hot spot. There were small flames licking up from underneath the charred ground, and we could see where the smoldering black spot had been working its way toward the house. The hose was a flexible coiled one, which made it hard to stretch over to where we needed it. I did my best not to trample these people's flower beds as I helped Wayne get the hose to the right location. The spigot was difficult, too, but I finally managed to get water flowing so Wayne could spray the area down.

"That was a bad one," he commented as he soaked the area. We would leave this particular hose right where it was. I expected to come back to this location at least a few times tonight. We didn't want this hot spot to flare back up. It was too close to the house.

It became very clear that these hot spots were going to be a problem. They were like land mines, quietly hidden in plain view, just waiting to be triggered. All it would take is some wind, and they could flare-up into full blown fires. One of these in the right location, flaring up at the right time, could take out the whole neighborhood. We had our work cut out for us, given the weather forecast for tonight.

After we finished, we returned to Viewpointe. Wayne headed out to work. I was pretty sure that instead of sleeping, he was here helping with Pointe Patrol. We'd periodically find him on the lawn by the café with his hat over his head, taking a quick cat nap. We all were sleep deprived and dragging, but I think Wayne's tank must have been the closest to empty, given the demands of his job at a time like this.

Aside from caring for our zones, we would also periodically do general patrols around the neighborhood for good measure. The more eyes we had on things, the better.

I made my way down toward the burned-out house on the corner. It wasn't nearly smoldering to the level that Per's house was, but it still didn't smell right, and Dave was pretty sure that things were hot underneath. It was a good spot to double-check, just in case something changed over there.

When I was about halfway to my destination, a truck pulled around the circle from behind me and parked on the other side of the street. It was a white flatbed pickup truck, with "Valley Fire" decals on both doors. The entire bed of the truck had been modified to hold a giant coil of thick hose. Half the hose was visible above the bed, and the other half was below, coiled on some sort of roller. The license plates were from Montana.

There were two people in the truck, a man and a woman, both wearing bright yellow jumpsuits. I stood by the passenger side, waiting for them to get out. The woman there seemed to be too busy to make eye contact and was arranging equipment. When she finally looked over, I smiled at her and she gave me a half smile back. She was pretty, but tired. It wasn't tired in the way that you look after a few long nights of work, but more tired in the way you look after having lived a difficult life. I could tell she didn't want to be here.

The man came out and around. He was much shorter than her and was friendly. He was clearly in charge, and she was his helper. I wondered if they were a couple.

"Hi there," he said. If he noticed my gun, which I'm sure he must have, he didn't give any indication. "We've been sent by insurance to make sure this house is all right." He gestured at the house behind him in the center of the circle.

"OK, there it is. Knock yourself out," I said. I turned and made my way back to my house.

I have to admit, I'm generally a pretty gullible person. I know this about myself. When I lived in Chicago, I was always getting scammed by people I'd run into on the street who gave me their sob story and needed help. I'd give them money to help with their drama and feel good about myself for doing so, until I realized (or usually until someone told me) that I had been duped.

"I drive a disabled girl in a wheelchair but just ran out of gas! The van is parked just behind that church. I need help!" one guy in particular told me as I was walking to work, completely beside himself with anxiety. Of course, I gave him what cash I had. Can't let the little girl in the wheelchair get stranded, after all! The weekend after that, I came across that same person at another street corner. I noticed he had a brand-new shirt on. He was telling anyone who would listen that he drove a van with a girl in a wheelchair but had run out of gas and needed help. *Again!* What were the odds?!

I think being overly honest myself and having a generally optimistic worldview, I tend to expect that others are the same and always believe the first thing that people tell me. It makes me a nice guy, but it also makes me pretty easy to trick. I'm getting better, but Laura has an infinitely more evolved bullshit detector, which comes in handy when she's around.

Luckily, the rest of Pointe Patrol isn't quite as trusting and showed up just after I walked away. They put more pressure on yellow jumpsuit man. They asked follow-up questions to test his story, which began to fall apart. He didn't know who lived in the house he had parked in front of, and he rattled off an address which happened to be Wayne's house, completely on the other side of the circle. The gang took pictures of both him and his truck. He didn't like that at all. He became belligerent, and the conversation quickly became heated.

Things may have escalated and become physical, but it was five against one, and he backed down and left when he realized belligerence wasn't going to work. He was a looter. I never expected them to show up in elaborate disguises, and now that I knew they would go to those lengths, there was no way I was going to be fooled again. I strongly suspect that had this guy showed up a couple days later, after we had a little more experience, we'd have had both him and his girlfriend duct-taped to a street lamp for the police. After this encounter, we became very territorial and aggressive toward anyone who showed up in the neighborhood unannounced.

An hour or so after the looters had driven away, I went back up to Fountainview to do a quick patrol. That's when I met Fountainview Mike for the first time. He and a fellow neighbor, Larry, were talking together, touring what was left of their street.

"How long have you been here?" he asked after I introduced myself.

"Since yesterday. We came back with our dog and spent the whole night patrolling for embers and looters."

"You brought your dog?"

"Yeah, Oscar. He's a Doberman. He was born to watch out for bad guys."

Mike studied me for a moment. "Nice. Go, Oscar."

We all chatted a bit, and I got both their phone numbers to make sure they were added to #VIEWPOINTE STRONG. Mike had heard about the effort being made by Pointe Patrol and wanted to be part of it. I told him to come visit us at the café when he had a chance or when he got hungry.

Mike and Larry had decided that they were going to hunt hot spots in the burned-out area of the neighborhood. This was actually a really large physical space. Although Fountainview was shaped like a *U*, there were many small side areas with houses tucked away. After it had all burned, what was left felt like a couple giant football fields full of rubble.

I wasn't sure how much a hot spot mattered in the middle of all that debris where there was nothing left to burn, but I wasn't an expert either, and putting out fires was what we were here to do, so I tried to be as encouraging as possible. Mike and Larry had scavenged a number of hoses that hadn't been prepped earlier and connected them into one really long hose, which they snaked through all the rubble. The two of them then made their way around, spraying down whatever smoldering areas they could find and chatting amiably as they went.

I didn't see a way I could help in the moment and didn't like being in the rubble due to the smell, so I only planned to stick around a little while. There was plenty of work to do if one needed a job. But before I had a chance to say my goodbyes, my attention was captured by a silver SUV cruising through the neighborhood.

I first saw it across the destruction toward Gardenview, and then it turned in and started down on Fountainview, driving slowly. I made my way out of the debris field as the SUV passed by and headed toward Viewpointe. *Another looter!?*

Although Dave had recommended we wear boots for protection, I preferred running shoes. I liked to be able to move quickly if I needed to and thought speed and mobility were worth the trade off in losing the protection boots offered. I took advantage of that decision and broke into a run back toward Viewpointe, one hand keeping the revolver at my side from flopping around too much.

I arrived just after the SUV passed the café and turned into the circle. There wasn't anyone else around. They were all off taking care of various tasks or taking naps.

I stood in the street in front of Gary's house, where the meeting had been earlier. No one could come in or out without passing through this spot, and I had a good view of half the circle from here. Unfortunately, the SUV was on the other side of the houses in the center, and I couldn't tell what it was doing. I hoped it hadn't stopped. Impatient, and not sure if I should stay or move, I waited to see if it would continue around the way it had come. Eventually it did, driving a little too slowly.

The car came back around toward where I was, and I approached diagonally from the driver's side. I thought the driver had probably seen me before and had no doubt that he saw me now. As he pulled up, he stopped and rolled his window down.

The SUV was driven by an older, heavyset person. He didn't look clean, and I immediately decided that he had been casing the neighborhood. What he said next only confirmed my suspicions.

"Have you seen the mail lady? She said she would deliver mail if she could, but I haven't been able to find her."

I was surprised by the question. *The mail?* What I felt like saying was something snarky, like *"Did you notice all these neighborhoods that have burned down? Do you think we're really paying attention to whether or not the mail has come??"* Instead, I only said, "No."

He looked at me, didn't say anything, and then drove away, heading down the hill. I had my phone ready and took a picture of his license plate as he left.

I sent a text to the group.

### #VIEWPOINTE STRONG

**ME:** Siver SUV with _____ license plate asking me if the mail lady came to deliver mail. Wtf? He drove around and then left. Just thought I'd report.

**BONNIE:** Clueless or fishing for who knows what

**ME:** I'm going for clueless

**BONNIE:** 😄

At around 4 p.m., Wayne texted the group with some good news.

**WAYNE:** I have Pizza and Chick-Fil-A enroute plus supplies

**TED:** Yum!

Five minutes later, Wayne showed up.

**WAYNE:** Come and get dinner

He had dropped everything off on the ever-growing pile of supplies in front of his house, and we all came out to get a piece of pizza. Fountainview Mike walked down and I introduced him to the rest of Pointe Patrol. The pizza was cold by the time I got any of it, but I didn't care. It was better than eating granola bars, which had been my plan up to that point.

When I saw Wayne, he told me he ran the plates I had reported on the silver SUV and that the car came back as belonging to someone on Gardenview, who had lost everything in the fire. He wasn't a looter after all; he was one of our neighbors. I had been wrong about him. Being suddenly homeless, and without any possessions, the guy had been overwhelmed and had chosen to try to complete whatever small task was in front of him that he was mentally and emotionally able to cope with, which had been trying to get his mail. I was suddenly glad I didn't say anything stupid to him when he asked about it.

Wayne only stuck around for a few minutes and was off again. He had two jobs: his regular one as a police officer and his new one as a member of Pointe Patrol. Both of those were full-time jobs that demanded overtime in the emergency, and Wayne gave the appearance of a man trying to squeeze thirty-six hours of work into a day that was only twenty-four hours long. I wondered if he had slept at all since the fire.

Mike headed back up to Fountainview to look for more hot spots with Larry, who was only up for the day, and others headed out to go deal with the ember in the woods that Sebastian, Eddie, and I had spotted in the night. Laura and I stuck around to watch the circle.

Shortly after everyone had disbursed, Wayne sent another text to #VIEWPOINTE STRONG. It was an alarming update.

**WAYNE:** URGENT UPDATE BE ON THE LOOKOUT Assholes in a U-Haul Trailer are looting nearby neighborhoods

**BONNIE:** Oh good lord

Bonnie was usually the first to respond to texts. I frequently thought she must have been sitting with her phone in hand to be as quick as she was.

This seemed serious. Being the only ones available in the circle, Laura and I decided that we'd guard it until others were able to make it back after doing their work. We had been taking a break at home when the message came though, so we leashed Oscar up and headed out. Due to his harness chafing him earlier, Oscar now only had to gear up with his usual two leashes.

We made our way over to Gary's lawn, and the three of us sat down, watching the entrance to the circle. I sent out an update to the group.

**ME:** We are at the entrance with the dog and a gun. We will deter them while the gang works

From our vantage point, we had a perfect view of Altruria. No one would be able to get into Viewpointe Circle, or even past the entrance, without us seeing them.

A few minutes after we sat down, we spotted two young men on mountain bikes as they cruised past. They were wearing dark clothes and had backpacks. They didn't slow as they passed but did look over. We made eye contact. Oscar growled. Neither side smiled or waved. *More looters?* There were all kinds of people coming through.

As I later learned, dealing with the ember in the woods turned out to be a huge adventure. Eddie, TJ, and Gary had gone down and found that the ember was actually up in a tree. It was higher than anyone could reach, and if it flared up, the whole tree could go, which would lead to the other trees going, too, and then the neighborhood. It was a dangerous ember.

Unbeknownst to them at the time, the woods were covered in poison oak. Poison oak is nasty. It doesn't have to be alive to get you. The oils remain potent for years, and all you really have to do is brush up against a dead branch to get them on your skin. The team at the tree had unknowingly tromped through tons of it on their way down the hill, a fact that would reveal itself shortly.

Eddie's grandfather had been a lumberjack, and Eddie spent some time helping him when he was younger. He had a plan to get up to the ember. He fastened a belt around his waist and looped the other side around the back of the tree. Then, using the same technique that technicians employ to climb telephone poles, he scaled the tree. He pushed upward sharply with his feet against the trunk, which temporarily loosened the belt, allowing him to scoot it up with his hands. Each hop got him farther up the trunk, and soon he was within reach of the burning branch.

He braced himself against the trunk by leaning against the belt and was able to create a stable base to work from in that way. He then took his hatchet and chopped the branch off. It was hard work, but they eventually got it down and were able to throw water on it to put it out. The cost was high in terms of effort, poison oak rash, and blisters, but it was one more source of potential destruction removed from the area.

Ten minutes or so after the update I had sent, Ted texted the group. He had been busy doing what he could on the outside to help.

> **TED:** Just talked to 911 and SRPD re looters—they're sending a patrol car

The police showed up a few minutes later.

> **ME:** Cops are here
>
> **BONNIE:**

The police car pulled up and stopped when they saw me. There were two officers sitting in the front seats, and the one on the passenger side had rolled his window down.

"Is everything OK?" he asked. I had been a little concerned about what would happen when the police saw me open carrying a firearm and took heart in the fact that they didn't seem to care.

"Yes. But there's a U-Haul full of looters cruising around here," I replied.

"We know. We're trying to find them." Then they were off. I was glad to see a police presence in the neighborhood. That would do a lot to secure the area.

Elliot texted next, changing the subject.

**ELLIOT:** Circle was just on NBC local news no interview

**TED:** From Vicky Nguyen on NBC We Investigate: "We had more to say but will run Eddie's interview later at 6 barring any breaking news"

Being without power and isolated behind police lines, no one at Pointe Patrol had any idea what was going on in the outside world without updates like this. I was glad to see that our neighborhood had made it to television. If people were aware that we were up here, hopefully that would help the next time we needed to call a fire truck.

**TED:** Let us know if you want us to call 911 & SRPD again!!!

**WAYNE:** We good

**WAYNE:** 2 gun toting fools and a kick ass dog... we good

**BONNIE:** 😁

**NORMA:** You guys are amazing!

**NICOLE:** Thanks and prayers to you all. It's so hard watching this unfold from afar but I am forever grateful. Big miracles are coming tonight! I just know it—and Hunter sends love too. He wants his crap back 😵🙏😵💕

Hunter is Wayne and Nicole's son and the youngest neighbor on

Viewpointe Circle. He was set to have an awesome Halloween this year, with the entire neighborhood to himself and no competition for treats.

**TED:** TV shows are made from this!! Harvey Weinstein working on a spaghetti western called "Wayne and Earik"

A few minutes later, Elliot gave us a weather update for tonight. Everyone was very concerned about the forecast for the wind in the early morning.

**ELLIOT:** Pointe Patrol: 2:30 to 7 a.m. worst of wind 15 miles per hour. ♥ you got this!

**BONNIE:** 👍

**DENISE:** This is Denise. I have the World's Best Neighbors!!!

**TED:** You GO Pointe Patrol!!!

**BONNIE:** 🙏🙏

The thread served a lot of purposes. The original reason was so that the neighbors could share important information quickly but what had become just as important was how it was being used to pull the community together. We had become a team. The constant encouragement, support, and humor the outside group sent to us over that thread was invaluable. It bolstered our spirits and gave us purpose. I think our texts back to them did the same. It gave them a window into the neighborhood, so they knew their homes were safe and protected.

# CHAPTER 8

# The Longest Night of My Life

AS THE SUN began to set, we all got ourselves psychologically ready for what might unfold. If we could get through this night, the neighborhood would probably survive. On the other hand, things could get very dicey, and it would all happen in the dark.

Laura and I had packed our emergency bags and left them by the door. My car was in the driveway, facing out. If the emergency call went out—someone driving two laps around the circle with their horn down—all that needed to be done was to grab the bags and the dog, throw them in the car, and go.

Laura and I both had keys to the car and the house. Unfortunately, the battery on one car key had died, so it didn't do a good job at locking or unlocking. Because of that, we decided to leave the car open for simplicity. Since there were looters around, neither one of us wanted to leave our valuables in an unlocked car, which is why they were by the door instead. If we had time, we'd be able to load up and go. If we didn't have time, we were prepared to leave the bags. It would depend on the situation. The main thing was that we got ourselves and Oscar out if the neighborhood was going up in flames.

I knew that I might spend long periods of time away from the house tonight and that Laura would be alone.

"If you hear the signal, and I'm not here, don't wait. Just go," I told her. "I'll catch up with you down the hill somewhere."

"OK."

"Do you have the keys?"

She reached up, feeling for the ribbon hanging from her neck to make sure.

"Yes."

As I mentioned before, Laura and I have different personalities. I'm a Virgo and like things to be precise. I like systems and routines. Keys always go in the same place, and I never change where that place is. That way, I can find them in the dark if I have to.

Laura is a Gemini, which is the opposite. She likes to change things up. When she first moved in with me, she drove me crazy by always moving the silverware to a different drawer. I could never find anything.

When I confronted her about it and told her that it was completely infuriating, she responded with, "Sorry, but it's my nature." Strangely, that made perfect sense to me in the moment, and since then I've been fine with her rearranging things. I like methods, and her method is to always change, so if I frame it like that, I understand it. I do think she might reconsider her urge to rearrange if she realized how many times I ask her where things are rather than trying to find them myself, but for the most part we've gotten used to our differences.

A habit much worse than moving the silverware was the trouble she had with keys. They were never in the same place twice. When we were dating, many times I'd show up to pick her up and would find her keys dangling out of the lock in her front door. You never knew where they might turn up.

In normal situations, none of that matters. It's kind of cute in a way. But in the situation we were in now, not being able to find the keys could be the difference between life and death. If the signal to leave came, it would happen in the dark, and things would be confusing and stressful. If I wasn't there, Laura needed to be able to get her keys immediately, without having to think about where they were.

Earlier in the day, it became clear the key situation might be an issue. We have a wooden bench by our front door, which became a sort of gear staging area. All the flashlights, gloves, masks, and associated equipment went on that bench. That way, when it was time to leave, everything we needed was at hand right in front of us. It worked well for me, and for Laura, too, for the most part, but she kept losing her house key. It would show up in the strangest places, and we'd have to conduct a fresh search for it every time we went out.

Realizing that this was a problem, our solution was to find a thick ribbon and make her a necklace. The house key and the car key went on that ribbon, and she wore them like jewelry. That way the keys would always be right there, hanging around her neck. As long as she wore the necklace it was impossible for her not to have access to the keys when she might need them. Her job was to keep that ribbon on all night, and my job was to be a pain in the rear and pester her about it.

I kissed her goodbye and headed out to meet Mike. It was cold, so I wore a down jacket. I had my black baseball cap on, which I had been wearing all day long. I had new batteries in my flashlight, work gloves stuffed into my back pockets, my mask hanging around my neck, and my revolver on my belt. I was as equipped for the night as I knew how to be. But the most important piece of equipment, by far, was my cell phone. That was my lifeline to Pointe Patrol.

I walked out of the circle and up Altruria to Fountainview where Mike was waiting. All the street lights were out. It was dark.

We met at his house. He had been getting ready. His car was parked in front with the back hatch open. He had a shovel thrown in there and had found five or six 3-gallon water jugs. We filled them up and loaded them into the back of his car. There was no way we could get hoses back into the rubble on the other side of Fountainview, so Mike's water jugs were perfect.

We set out on foot, walking the perimeter of the burn zone. We started off on the fence line between Viewpointe and Fountainview, making our way back down the line between the two neighborhoods and then over to the right on the Fountainview side.

I wore my mask for this part, as that sulfur smell was strong. It felt like being an ant walking through a camp fire. We picked our way through what had been people's houses, stumbling over ash and trying to be careful not to step on anything sharp. I wondered if I would have to throw my shoes away after this was all done—they were covered in soot.

As we came back through the middle of the *U* area that is Fountainview, we stumbled upon our first hot spot. It looked like a smoldering orange glow under the ash, and we poked at it with a piece of debris to open it up. It seemed almost like a pile of old phone books that hadn't burned.

We marked the spot and drove back up in Mike's car. He got as close as he could without running over glass or other sharp objects, which were scattered everywhere. It took three or four of the water jugs, but we managed to extinguish the hot spot. It hissed as we poured water over it.

It was very clear that we weren't going to last long if we had to carry these jugs too far. They weren't heavy over the short run, but carrying them over distances where the footing was unstable was a challenge. I was already tired to start with, and my body felt like jelly, so doing a whole lot of physical work was going to be difficult. Mike was a lot fresher, having only come up today.

"You don't look so good…. Maybe I should be the one carrying the gun," he joked.

I laughed. I knew I was dragging. I had only slept one night since the evacuation, and that had been the awkward night spent in Judith's bed, which had been way too small.

We drove the car up the remaining part of Fountainview and parked it near the end. We then headed out to scout on foot. We were going to keep the car close by and would use it to haul the water as much as possible. I could see how the back end of it squatted down under the weight of the water jugs.

We didn't find any more hot spots on Fountainview, although we made a thorough search. It was all burned out. Once we got to the end, we headed across the street to check out the area between the apartments and Altruria. There was a large area between the sidewalk and the actual apartment complex, which was comprised of a number of large buildings. Tall bushes ran the entire length of the street down past the entrance to Viewpointe, and they had been trimmed to create a sort of natural wall and divider. On the other side of those bushes was a creek, and the ditch was quite deep. There were a lot of areas for embers to hide.

We started at the top, at the parking lot just before the creek started to form. There were plant beds there, and I spotted a smoldering patch in the mulch about three feet in diameter. It was easy to see in the dark, as the edges glowed orange. Thin wisps of silver smoke made their way up from the ground.

Mike went to move the car and drove it right into the entrance of the parking lot, stopping there. He opened the back, and we prepared to get a couple jugs out. That's when the police showed up.

There were three police cars, each equipped with bright floodlights. They drove up to us fast, coming to an abrupt stop behind Mike's car. I noticed that they blocked us in. If we were looters planning to make a run for it, there was no way to get out now.

Six police officers approached and surrounded us. *Oh shit. Here we go!* I froze. I wasn't going to move or cause them any concern until they knew what was what. Although I stood calmly with my arm over my gun, blocking it, I had no doubts that they could see it.

"Do you live around here?" the lead officer asked me.

"Yes. I live on Viewpointe Circle, which is three streets down, and Mike lives on Fountainview, which is right there. Our houses survived. We are part of a group that stayed to protect the neighborhood after the fire."

I noticed that the police had arranged themselves around me in a circle. One officer had taken the lead, so he was the one I was speaking to, but it was clear that I was surrounded on all sides. I also noticed that none of them stood directly across from any of the others. That was probably in case they needed to start shooting.

The other thing they did was that they got a little too close. No one likes to be surrounded, especially by an armed group of police officers. But surrounding someone, and then stepping in, is a good way to apply psychological pressure. I was sure this pressure was done on purpose, so that they could see how I reacted under stress. It was the same sort of thing that Pointe Patrol started to do with looters. Put some stress on them and see what happens. I had some adrenaline going, so I was thinking pretty fast and making mental notes of their tactics as they were applying them. Presumably, in the police academy, you learn about how to do all this stuff. I was learning it in the moment by going through it. Being the suspect is not a comfortable role to have to play. I wasn't tired anymore. I was completely awake and alert.

"There are nine of us that stayed," I continued. "We're working with a retired firefighter and a SWAT officer." I then told them Dave and Wayne's full names, hoping they would recognize them.

"We're not from the area, so I don't know who that is," the police officer told me, referring to Wayne. Another one from my left asked, "What unit is he with? Are you working through dispatch?"

I actually didn't know anything about Wayne's job. All I heard was that he helped out with SWAT. In that moment, for reasons I didn't understand, I answered "LAPD," and immediately regretted it. I think it just popped out of my mouth. Obviously, I've watched too many police shows on television involving the LAPD. We were a long way from Los Angeles, and there was no way Wayne worked for LAPD.

I quickly corrected myself.

"No, wait. Not LAPD. Actually, I'm not sure who he works with. He's my neighbor. Can I text him and get him up here to explain?"

I got my phone and sent a text to the Pointe Patrol thread.

## Pointe Patrol

**ME:** Wayne need help with cops

**ME:** Fountainview and Altruria

I then continued my explanation. "Our area was declared a burn zone, which means they aren't going to send any fire trucks. We tried calling today, but they wouldn't help. There have been looters coming through here all day long. We're really concerned about the wind picking up tonight and are trying to go and put out all the hot spots we can find. We've broken into teams. Mike and I are taking care of this area up here, and everyone else is back in the circle watching their own sections."

Mike then took that opportunity to grab a water jug and make his way through the crowd over to the burning area. He poured the water out over the hot spot, being careful to soak it all, and then covered dirt over the top. All the rest of us watched him as he did it.

I saw the cops glance at each other. One of them, off to my right, made a face and looked down, shaking his head. There was more than one conversation going on. The cops had all been having their own private one this whole time. They had been trying to decide what to do with us, and as a group, they seemed to have come to a decision.

A different officer than the one I had spoken with now stepped up. "We know you're just trying to save your neighborhood. We're here now, and we're going to be here all night." The pressure that they had been applying this whole time suddenly pulled back. They were going to let us go. I felt relief flood my body.

"Thanks," I told this new officer. "I'm really glad you guys are up here. So I'll let you handle security then, and we'll just worry about finding fires."

That was the closest we came to discussing my gun. I didn't want to bring it up, because I thought that if I did then we'd have to have a conversation about it. I think they probably felt the same way. Once it was declared and out in the open, then they'd have to be police officers and would have to investigate it, and I'd have to be the guy wearing a gun in an evacuation zone after curfew. So they didn't ask, and I didn't volunteer.

Mike and I didn't look or act like looters. The car was full of water bottles, not stolen electronics. And they caught us putting out an active hot spot. Ultimately, they probably would be doing the exact same thing if they were in our shoes, guns and all, and everyone sort of knew it.

Mike and I went back to his car, and as soon as I got in I loosened my belt and took the gun off. That had been intense! I decided I wasn't going to wear it anymore. The odds of getting harassed by the cops were much higher than the odds of needing it against a looter, and I didn't want to have to go through that again. Besides, now that there was a police presence here, maybe the looters wouldn't be an issue.

Wayne had never showed up. He wasn't present in the neighborhood just then and had been off dealing with an emergency of his own.

### Pointe Patrol

**ME:** Never mind. We're cool

**ME:** Cops are patrolling all night

The police got back in their cars, and we watched the convoy head down the street and turn into Viewpointe Circle. They were probably going to check out our story.

Mike and I took a few minutes and decompressed in the car before getting out to walk down Altruria. I left my revolver tucked under the passenger seat.

Before the bushes get thick and the ditch gets steep, there's a grassy patch that slopes down into the creek. It wasn't grassy now, but black and charred. In the middle, a black cat sat there and looked at us. We shined our light on him, but he didn't seem concerned. He actually seemed quite content to be hanging out in the middle of that field.

This was the first of many strays that I would encounter over the next few days. When people had evacuated, some of them had done so when their cats had been out. Those cats were now stranded and lost. It was not uncommon to come across a house that was burned to the foundation and to find that someone had erected a makeshift shelter with water and food bowls. Weeks later, a massive volunteer cat-trapping brigade sprouted up, and they caught and returned many of the strays to their people, including this one.

I wondered if I should try to catch that cat but wasn't sure if I'd be able to, so I hesitated. Looking back, I probably should have, but in the moment it didn't seem like the right thing to do. I would end up meeting his owner days later—their house had burned, and he had no home to return to. For now, he was scavenging around the apartments.

We slowly walked down the sidewalk, stopping every few feet to peer behind the bushes. The unmistakable glow of embers brought us to a halt, and we fought our way through the brambles and halfway down the embankment to come across what was left of a burning tree trunk resting on its side.

Mike went back and pulled up the car, and the two of us hauled the water jugs down the hill to extinguish the embers. It was steep, and dark. This would be an easy place to twist an ankle or trip over something.

After we had finished, we were beat. It was time for a break. We each went back home and planned to reconnect in half an hour or so. We wanted to walk the entire length of that creek and investigate both sides of it. We were certain there were more embers to discover.

It was getting toward 10 p.m. when Wayne returned. The gang had hooked up Joe and Carmen's generator in the backyard of the café, and someone had plugged in a high-powered construction light. Eddie's driveway was as bright as day, and the light illuminated half the neighborhood. I was able to see the glow from inside my house. It was a welcome sight, and potential looters would definitely steer clear when they saw it.

Wayne took a picture of the lights and our neighborhood behind it, and then attached it to his post. That would be comforting to the outside group. They took the opportunity to say goodnight to us and wished us well.

## #VIEWPOINTE STRONG

**WAYNE:** #VIEWPOINTE STRONG tonight.

**RHONDA:** Thank you all. Be safe 🖤

**SHERI:** You all are awesome! Thank you and be safe!

**NORMA:** Thank you for taking such good care of the Circle. Have a peaceful night.

**ME:** Mike (Fountainview resident) and I got surrounded by 8 cops on our last run. This place seems pretty secure 😜

I think I may have exaggerated the number. My memory says there were three cars, so that probably results in six cops rather than eight. I don't think any of them would want to ride in the back where the criminals go, which is the only way there could have been more than six of them there.

I came home and crashed on the couch. I told Laura about my adventure with the police. She thought maybe I should keep wearing the gun around anyway, but I felt a little like I'd been lucky. A different group of cops might have treated the situation another way. Besides, if there were that many cops cruising the neighborhood, I didn't think looters would be poking around much. It would not be safe for them.

I did think it was funny that Laura liked the idea of me wearing a gun around. This was a far cry from the Laura of years past who didn't even want one in the house.

# CHAPTER 9

# Saving The Boulders

SEBASTIAN TEXTED TO the Pointe Patrol thread to check in.

### Pointe Patrol

**SEBASTIAN:** Hey Earik and Mike, are you guys doing ok?
We're brewing some coffee if all is good

*Coffee!* It was 10 p.m., way past the time when I can drink coffee and expect to get any sleep, but this wasn't a night when I planned on sleeping much.

There have only been a couple times in my life where I've stayed up more than one night in a row. It's not something I like to do regularly. In all the times I've had to do it, I've noticed that I get really tired the first night, but then after that my body somehow loses track of its internal clock. And at that point, rather than wanting to sleep, I mostly just feel like jelly. I had definitely entered that wobbly, gelatinous stage.

**ME:** We're about to do a run up there

**ME:** Where's the coffee at? I'm dragging

**FOUNTAINVIEW MIKE:** Earik and I took a short break. We are supposed to meet up again and do some rounds in a couple minutes. Thanks for checking

**EDDIE:** Coffee here

**EDDIE:** Got the generator going too

I made my way over to the café, and the gang was all there. Mike had beat me there and was chatting with a couple other people.

I made my way in and found the coffee maker, which was brewing next to a stack of clean cups that someone had brought out. The generator was running in the backyard and the hum of the engine was loud yet not unwelcome. Two thick extension cords, one of which I recognized as mine, came in through the back door of the garage, which was cracked open. One cord snaked over to the right side of the garage, and the other went up the stairs into the house.

Eddie had a work desk in the garage where he kept his computer, and he had a number of long power strips along the wall behind it. These were now powered on, and there were a cluster of cell phones plugged into them. All different kinds of phone cords and adapters were arranged nearby. I found a spare cord and plugged my phone in next to the others. Being able to charge cell phones was a big deal. This had been a constant issue. The other extension cord that ran into the house was for the refrigerator. Thanks to Joe and Carmen's generator, we now had lights, the ability to charge phones, and a way to keep food fresh. This was a huge step up from earlier that day.

While I waited for my phone to build up a healthy charge, I drank coffee and checked in with the group. The three police cars had come down into the circle, and the police had gotten out and talked with everyone.

"They gave me a ton of trouble about my hatchet," Eddie said. Eddie wore it around on his belt for easy access.

"'What's that?'" Eddie said, imitating a police officer questioning him suspiciously in a low voice.

"'A hatchet.'

"'What's it for?'

"'I use it to put out fires.'"

Eddie had used it earlier in the day when he and the others had put out the embers in the tree. We laughed, and I filled him in on the details about my experiences with those same police officers earlier.

Afterward, I couldn't get the fact that they had questioned him about his hatchet out of my head. Clearly, they were concerned that it was being used as a weapon and not as a tool. But I had been wearing a gun. How does one put out a fire with a gun? Eddie had been at his house, with a generator running and a bunch of neighbors around him. I had been up the street where I didn't belong, creeping around in the dark after curfew. But he got questioned, and I didn't.

What was the difference? I didn't want to think it had come down to race, but that's the most obvious (and most uncomfortable) answer to the question.

What if I had been a black guy? Would the police have let things go as easily? How many black men have been shot and killed in similar situations? Their deaths have been all over the news, and there have been enough of them to spawn the #BlackLivesMatter movement. I had a firearm out in the open and had rummaged in my pocket for my phone to text Wayne. I'd like to think that it was my good looks and charming personality that put the police at ease, but how much of my charming personality has to do with me being a white guy? What if it had been TJ out there with the gun? Would the young Latino guy in the flat-brimmed hat with the revolver have been treated as gently? I don't know.

Chip, one of Wayne's friends from work, had come up with him, and both of them were wearing brown uniforms with "Sheriff" printed in bold letters on the back. We were glad for their presence, especially if there were going to be a lot of police patrols coming through.

After we drank our coffee, Mike and I headed out to finish looking for embers in the ditch on the other side of Altruria. We thought we'd start off on this end and work our way back up toward the top of the hill where we had left off earlier in the night. We exited the circle and headed right.

We made it down about halfway toward Miramonte, then turned around and headed back up the hill. The best way to look for embers is without flashlights, so we did almost everything in the dark. The flashlights were really only used in case we thought there was something we might trip over.

We worked at an easy pace, and the coffee was definitely helping. I didn't feel like I was dragging anymore; I was much more alert and energetic. We probably had only been gone ten minutes before another police car came up the hill, slowing down as it approached us.

The spotlights were turned on and pointed at us, which made it impossible for me to see anything. I smiled into the light and waved. Mike probably did the same, although I wasn't looking at him so am not certain. It was pretty clear by that point that we didn't fit whatever stereotypes the police have for looters. Mike's a dermatologist and I'm a software guy, and we both look and act like it. I think we'd have to try pretty hard to give anyone a vibe that we were up to no good.

The spotlights dimmed, and the car pulled forward so we could look through the passenger side window. There was only one officer in the car, older than the six that had surrounded us earlier. He gave off an air of being a higher rank than the others.

"Are you the two guys from before?" he asked.

"Yeah—we're looking for burning logs in the ditch," I said.

"Find any?"

"Yes!" we both said, thinking of the log just up the hill that we had put out.

The cop smiled and drove off. I'm glad they all knew about us now. It would make things easier. This had been the most police I had seen up here since I had been back. It had been sort of a no man's land in the beginning. Now things were the opposite. It felt like we were on lockdown.

There are two entrances into the Boulders apartment complex. One is just below Viewpointe, and the other is up the hill toward Fountain-view. The ditch and bushes stretch between them and are thickest right in the middle.

We had made it to the first entrance to the Boulders, below Viewpointe, and turned in. We thought that it might be easier to see what was down in the ditch if we worked our way up from this side, rather than from the street side. There was no wall of bushes here, only some trees and whatever grew naturally.

We made our way in past a thick grove of blackberry bushes. I tried to be careful so that the thorns wouldn't snag my down jacket. Down jackets and thorns are a pretty bad combination. I was ahead of Mike and the first to spot the flicker of embers.

We worked our way in and found more than just embers. As we made it toward the bottom of the creek, where we could look down the steepest part of the hill, we saw live flames. These embers had been smoldering away for days, and this was the moment when they went from smoldering to full-on burning. The flames were two feet high and growing. These trees hadn't burned yet, so there was plenty of fuel for the fire if it got any bigger.

I pulled out my phone, getting ready to text Pointe Patrol, but at that moment Wayne appeared on the other side of the creek from where we were. He had seen flashlights and had come over to check it out in case we were looters. We were almost directly across the entrance to Viewpointe Circle, so it had been a short walk for him.

"Home team?" he called out from his position at the sidewalk. He wasn't able to see the flames from where he stood.

"Home team!" I yelled back. "We've got fire! We need buckets!"

I think Wayne could sense the urgency and disappeared from view, hurrying back. Mike stayed to mark the spot, and I left to reconnect with the rest of Pointe Patrol and help direct them to the fire.

As I made it back to the entrance to the circle, I passed Gary, who was running at top speed with a bucket full of water back toward where I had come from. From the way he moved, I could tell that the bucket must have been filled to the top. Mike was signaling where to go with his flashlight. The rest of the group was filling buckets and loading them onto Sebastian's truck, which was parked in front of Wayne's house.

Sebastian and a few guys drove the truck over and parked it right next to where Gary and a few others had pushed through the bushes to get down to the fire. Buckets were passed down from the truck to people closer to the fire at the bottom. The fire had begun to put off quite a bit of light of its own, and the location couldn't be missed. Mike and I had stumbled on to it at exactly the right time. Ten minutes later and we'd have had a huge problem.

I made my way through the bushes and tried to make myself useful. There weren't any more buckets to carry, so I stood back and shined light to prevent anyone from tripping over anything. Wayne and Chip were right in the middle of it, fighting the flames. We made progress, and soon the flames died down, retreating back to their embers.

At that moment, a police car pulled up. I couldn't see the street from where I was on the other side of the bushes, but the blue and red lights were unmistakable. Dave had remained up by the truck, and I heard him talking to the officers in his low voice. I couldn't hear what they were saying but could guess how the conversation was going.

Wayne called up to them, "I'm with the sheriff's department. I'll come up there in a minute so you can verify." The fire wasn't completely out, and the team was still shoveling dirt onto what was left of the embers.

I looked up to see two police officers making their way down to where we were. They hadn't wanted to wait. These officers were younger than many of the others I had met tonight, and they didn't seem nearly as hardened as the six that I had interacted with earlier. They stopped and took in the situation, clearly noticing Wayne and his friend in their uniforms.

"Hey there," Wayne said in a friendly tone. "Who are you guys with?"

"Santa Rosa," one of the officers replied. These were local boys.

Wayne paused. "Oh… well, in that case, fuck you."

All the rest of us froze, not used to anyone speaking to police like that. Wayne appeared to be enjoying himself. The two officers seemed to have been surprised themselves, and one of them snorted. The other reached up and brushed his shoulder off in an angry gesture. *This must be cop humor*, I thought to myself, although there was no way I was going to laugh out loud.

They stayed a while longer, then eventually turned around and left. "If you're with him, I guess you don't have to worry about curfews," one of them told us on the way out. The flashing lights went out, and I heard them drive off.

"That was a good find, you fuckers," Wayne said to Mike and me when the fire was out. Mike and I stayed at the site, intending to continue our patrol. There was still a lot of area to check.

The rest of Pointe Patrol returned the way they had come, taking the shovels and empty buckets with them. They would go back and prep the truck so that it would be ready in case we needed it again. Wayne was the last to leave and turned around when he reached the sidewalk.

"Good find, fuckers," he repeated again with emphasis. We understood being called "fuckers" was a term of endearment from Wayne and took it as such. We raised our hands in salute and turned to continue our search.

As we made our way up the creek, walking along the edge on the Boulders' side, the trees got bigger and the embankment got steeper. We didn't come across any embers until we were almost to the next parking lot.

We spotted them on the other side, down almost to the bottom of the creek. It would be difficult to get down there. We scanned the area with our flashlights and realized that this was the same spot we had visited earlier tonight, when we had found the burning log. The log we had put out had been a branch that had broken off a huge tree that had caught fire. What we were looking at now was the main trunk. It had fallen across the creek bed, and the entire underside of it was glowing orange.

I texted Pointe Patrol.

## Pointe Patrol

**ME:** We have another one

**LAURA:** Fire?

Laura was at home, and I hadn't filled her in on details since I had seen her last. She didn't know what was going on out here.

**WAYNE:** Enroute

The bushes were very thick by the sidewalk on Altruria and made it difficult to get in from that side. Mike and I found a natural doorway earlier, where the branches parted enough to allow access to the embankment. That would be the ideal spot for the rest of the team to get in with the buckets.

Mike made his way down to the creek bed to investigate further, and I went back up and around to show Pointe Patrol where to go. I only had to wait a moment before I saw headlights pull out of Viewpointe Circle and head up the road toward me. Sebastian's pickup had officially become our fire truck. I turned my flashlight on so they would see where I was.

Getting buckets down the embankment was dangerous. It was steep, and the ground was slick. More than one of us had our feet slide out from under us on the way down. There were a lot of boulders and logs at the bottom of the creek, which made it difficult to find a place to stand.

I made my way down with a bucket of water, inching my way to where the others were, and passed the bucket over to them. There wasn't a good place to stand down by the tree, so I waited on the edge of the circle to see what was happening.

The problem was that all the embers were on the underside of the tree trunk, and there was no easy way to get to them. The trunk itself was massive and stretched all the way across the creek. There was no way to move it. It was too heavy.

Chainsaws were called for, and one of them was brought down from where it had been stored in the truck. These were small chainsaws, much more suited to cutting branches and small trees than cutting through fallen trunks, but it was all we had.

Wayne was the closest to the tree, and he ended up getting the chainsaw. Chip was positioned on the other side of the trunk and shined a light down where Wayne began cutting. I moved up behind Wayne and shined my light right over his shoulder onto the same spot. Others added their lights, and for the most part we were able to keep Wayne from cutting anything in the dark that he couldn't see.

The blade of the chainsaw was too short to cut the trunk in one pass, so it took multiple attempts from different angles to finally get through. When the trunk finally gave way, Chip had to jump back to dodge it. It went crashing down onto the rocks below and rolled off to rest at the bottom of the creek bed. No one wanted to get hit with a five-hundred-pound log just then. We were trying to be as careful as possible, all things considered.

Once the trunk was cut, we were able to access the area underneath and found that there was a nest of embers there, far more extensive than we had thought. Had the wind picked up and blown low enough to fan these embers, this could easily have turned into something completely out of control. That was two bullets dodged in the ditch that night.

After we had saturated the area with water, we all scrambled back up the steep embankment and regrouped at the truck. As before, Mike and I stayed back while everyone else returned to Viewpointe.

The two of us finished our sweep of the rest of the creek area, glad to find no other embers or hot spots. We then worked our way back from the upper parking lot of the Boulders to the lower one. Everything looked good.

By now, we were both wiped out and decided that this was a good time to stop for a couple hours. We agreed to do another patrol at around two in the morning. I headed into the circle, and Mike walked toward Fountainview.

Laura and I both had a fitful sleep the previous night. When we bought our couch, we got something that was perfect for sitting up: nice, firm cushions and a slightly narrow seat. It couldn't be beat for having a conversation or for having guests over. However, these same qualities made it terrible for sleeping. It's too narrow and too hard. I've taken my share of naps on it, but last night had been awful. Now that Pointe Patrol was organized, and we had an evacuation signal arranged, we felt that it wouldn't be too irresponsible of us to try to get some sleep in an actual bed, with regular pillows and covers.

I set the alarm on my phone to wake me up at the appropriate time and put it on the nightstand. I had brought the lantern up, as well as the gun. Oscar came and guarded the doorway. He would be a bad thing for a would-be looter to accidentally trip over in the night.

As I arranged the pillows and got ready for a few hours of sleep, I noticed a light coming from Miramonte. That was unusual because Miramonte had become a black hole in the night. I looked out the window and saw a police car positioned right at the entrance to that neighborhood, and it had floodlights pointed in all directions. The officers in the car would periodically sweep through the rubble with a spotlight, which was incredibly bright. I could see everything they shined it on from my vantage point up on the hill. That police car would remain there the entire night, guarding the neighborhood. I definitely felt safer knowing there was a sentry down there.

I got under the covers and felt my body relax. I still had the effects of the coffee running through my system, but I didn't feel like that would stop me from sleeping. This was the first time I had been back in my own bed since the evacuation three nights ago, and it felt good to be home, even if it was under difficult circumstances.

Before I could fall asleep, my phone started vibrating. A text message had come through. I reached over and grabbed it to see who it was. I had become a teenager the past few days, obsessively checking my phone for texts.

### Pointe Patrol

**WAYNE:** Need water buckets up at the Apartments

**EDDIE:** Copy

I put the phone back down. Wayne had found something at the Boulders. Another text came through, and I picked the phone back up.

**WAYNE:** Shovels

**WAYNE:** Uphill toward Fountainview

I was sure that most of Pointe Patrol was still up. They had all been at the café when I went home, and that hadn't been very long ago. There were plenty of them there, and I knew they would be able to handle this without me. I felt it might be better for me to get some rest now so that I could relieve them a couple hours later and give them a break. Besides, I was already under the covers, and I needed to rest from all the wandering around I had done with Mike.

I put the phone back down and covered myself back up. I was lying flat on my back with my eyes closed, which is how I usually fall asleep. Once I get tired enough in that position, I flip to the side and pass out. I was having a little trouble getting to that point, though. It might have been the effects of the coffee that made it hard or my concern about Wayne's texts. Part of me kept thinking that maybe I should get up and go check on things. I had that tingling feeling where something just didn't feel right.

My phone was silent for half an hour. Then, at 1 a.m., another set of texts came through the Pointe Patrol thread.

**WAYNE:** Buckets same place almost

**WAYNE:** Hurry!

*Crap!* This didn't sound good. So much for sleeping.

"I've got to go. They found something," I told Laura. I located my clothes pile on the floor and started putting everything back on. My jeans were dirty; I could feel the grit on them. I was tying my shoelaces when the next text came.

**WAYNE:** Turn in, this one's bad. Need fire extinguishers

I was out the door and jogged over to the café. The big floodlights were on, and I saw Dave sitting in a chair, checking his phone. Everyone else was gone.

I went out to Altruria and hurried up the hill toward the second parking lot to the Boulders, where I had been surrounded by police earlier that night. I found the team there, next to the first building in the apartment complex.

The apartments were multiple stories. At the second floor, the buildings extended outward, which created a three- or four-foot overhang. There was a medium-sized pine tree planted next to the corner of the building, and the top of it was very close to the overhang. The mulch that surrounded the tree was smoldering.

The gang was milling about, exploring the smoldering area. As I walked around the backside of the tree, I could see that the hot spot completely surrounded the tree by a good five feet on all sides. It was completely covered in embers—and they were starting to light up. The base of the tree had already started to burn. The path that the fire would take was obvious to everyone. First the tree would light up, then the fire would jump to the overhang, and this first apartment building would catch. After that, all the rest of them would go, and probably all the surrounding areas as well, including Viewpointe. It was bad.

"How did you find this?" I asked Wayne once I got my bearings.

"I was up here earlier and knew about it. I thought I'd drive by to check up on it and found it like this," he explained. "I've already called 911. They're sending a fire truck."

This would be a hard one to put out with buckets. The smoldering area was huge, and it would take a lot of trips down to Viewpointe for refills.

While we were waiting for the fire truck, I went over to the building, thinking that maybe there would be a water spigot there. I found one, but it didn't have a regular knob. Instead, it had some sort of nut that fit into a proprietary knob that only maintenance must have access to. It was clear that the Boulders didn't want any of their residents accessing the water spigots on the outside of the buildings.

"Come on. Where are they?" Wayne was getting impatient. There was no sign of the fire truck, and the smoldering was getting worse by the minute. I went over to talk to a couple of the guys.

"If we had a hose and pliers, we might be able to turn the water on," I suggested.

Eddie agreed. He had been thinking the same thing. "I bet I could do it with a pair of needle-nose pliers."

"OK. I'm going to run back and get pliers and a hose," I said. It would be great if the fire truck showed up, but it wasn't clear that we had a lot of time to wait. We needed to do something if we could, even if it was just to buy the firefighters more time.

I took off, sprinting out of the parking lot and down the hill. I suspected I might need to run somewhere at some point, and it looked like I had been right. For the second time, I was glad I was wearing running shoes instead of boots. I'm in pretty good shape and was able to move quickly down the hill. I wondered what the police would think if they pulled around the corner just then to see a guy sprinting down the hill toward them with a flashlight.

I made it back to Viewpointe and ran into the circle. Dave was standing out toward the front of Eddie's driveway, watching me.

"I need a pair of needle-nose pliers!" I yelled at him as I ran past. He nodded and turned around to rummage in Eddie's garage.

I made it back to my house and went over to the side yard where we have a big black hose. It's not a regular hose, but the kind that expands and contracts as water is added. Those kinds of hoses tend to be fragile, and I had returned the first two we had purchased due to them springing leaks. This one was a redesigned model, which I had bought with suspicion. But it held up well the last few months, and I was pleasantly surprised with its performance. It was very light, so it was easy to carry and move around, and it also had an awesome built-in nozzle that could shoot water a long distance with a lot of force.

I unscrewed it from the wall as fast as I could and gathered it up into my arms. I then unlocked the side door to the garage and rushed inside. I went to a drawer where I keep a lot of pliers and similar tools and grabbed two different kinds, both a needle-nose set as well as a larger vice-grip pair, just in case.

I ran out to the car and threw the supplies in. Without buckling the seat belt, I flew out of the driveway. I spotted Chip waiting in the road in front of the café, with Dave on the other side of the street. I pulled up between them and stopped, letting Chip get in.

I waved to Dave, signaling that I found everything I needed, and once Chip had closed his door, I drove out of the circle and sped up the hill to the group. I made my way into the lot and parked just above where the team was waiting, in the closest spot that was out of the way of the roundabout we were next to. There was no fire truck yet, and I didn't want to block them when they showed up. We didn't know it at the time, but the fire truck wouldn't be coming—they had already been rerouted to a more pressing situation.

The two of us jumped out, and I gave the hose to Gary. I then offered both sets of pliers to Eddie, holding them out in the flat of my palms. He picked the needle-nose ones out and made his way over to the water spigot.

Eddie and Gary messed around with the spigot together, and soon they had water flowing through the hose. The spigot was relatively close to the tree, and the hose could really stretch out, so we quickly had water flowing right onto the smoldering embers.

The mulch was deep, and the hottest embers were below the surface.

We found that just spraying the top of the mulch didn't put them out. To really extinguish them, the area needed to be raked over to expose the embers hiding underneath. The more severe the hot spot was, the deeper the embers were. So in order to completely put the area out required a lot of raking and spraying. Burning mulch is stubborn.

Once we had the tree under control, we began checking the surrounding area. Whoever landscaped the Boulders had gone completely crazy with mulch, and it was everywhere. It was around each building and in all of the common areas between them. We were in an ocean of mulch and had begun to realize how dangerous it was. Sebastian found another smoldering area just down the pedestrian walkway, between the building we were at and the next one over.

It was too far away for the hose, so we had to look for another spigot. We finally came across one halfway around the building, past where Sebastian's spot was. Loosening the nut that released the water wasn't easy. It took two people to do it, one to hold the light, and the other to use the pliers. Eddie became the official pliers operator, and the rest of us took turns helping with the light.

Getting water flowing from the second spigot was more difficult than the first, and Eddie struggled to loosen the nut. Wayne was impatient.

"I'll give you some water," he said, unzipping his fly and taking a piss on the nearest hot spot.

Not realizing what he was doing, I turned and shined my flashlight right on him, putting everything right in the spotlight for everyone to see. I quickly moved the light away, but it was too late—we all had a good look at what he was up to and started laughing. When we told Dave about it the next day, he responded with the wisdom gained from his decades of experience as a professional firefighter: "You aren't the first person to piss on a fire, and you certainly won't be the last."

Eddie had gotten the hose working, and the hot spots were being dealt with. These were just small ones, and it only took a couple people to work each one. As the rest of the crew raked and watered the spots, I wandered further down the path, scanning for more smoldering areas.

I found the next one twenty or thirty feet away, around the other side of the first building and up a flight of steps. It was a medium-sized patch. I went back and signaled to the group.

For whatever reason, there was a water leak nearby, and water was shooting out of the ground into a giant puddle. It must have been caused by embers that had burned through the automatic sprinkler lines. We had to jump over the water to get to the new location.

While the other two hot spots were being dealt with, Gary came over and helped with the new one. He simply took one of the buckets we had brought, filled it up in the big puddle, and then carried it up the stairs to extinguish the embers. I searched along the wall and helped direct him to the different locations.

At this point, I ended up stepping into the role as the spotter and would range ahead of the group looking for hot spots. As I'd find them, I'd remember the location and go back to escort the team forward when they were available.

The hot spots were numerous, and it didn't take long before we lost count of how many we had extinguished. The embers were everywhere, and the mulch was the perfect environment for them to smolder in. The Boulders was an ember nursery.

When I made it to the third and fourth buildings, things got more difficult because there were no more spigots. That meant that in order to get water, the team would have to haul buckets from the puddle area, or from the nearest spigot. Water is heavy. You can carry a bucket or two without any trouble, but doing it over and over again in the middle of the night, after being up for a couple days in a row, was completely exhausting. The pace began to slow, and I frequently found myself outside the line of sight of the group as I searched for other hot spots.

The Boulders was constructed at the bottom of a huge hill. The hill was much taller than any of the apartments and towered over it. The fire looked like it had burned all the way down the hill, as it was completely black. One thing that the property managers had done well was to keep the grass on that hill trimmed short at all times. They had actually brought goats in from time to time, and the goats roamed across the hill, naturally trimming the grass down to the roots. Had those goats not done their jobs, there would have been more fuel to burn on the hill, and the fire would have been much stronger and hotter as it rushed down toward the Boulders. I'm not sure the apartments would have made it in that case. All things considered, we all might owe the survival of our homes to those goats!

As I found myself alone in the back of the Boulders, I couldn't help but notice how easy it would be to loot these apartments. The hill provided perfect cover from the back side, and the apartments on the ground floor had sliding glass doors that you could just walk right up to. All you would need is a way to cut a hole in the glass (or a big rock), and you'd be in. If someone knew what they were doing, they'd easily be able to clean out all the ground floor apartments in an hour or two. I was happy that I didn't see any signs of break-ins but knew that if any would-be looters were familiar with the area, this would definitely be an enticing spot.

I came upon a dense group of tall foxtail ferns, which sprung up from the ground in long thick shoots. The entire garden was smoking. Some of the plants were no longer green, having turned gray from being burned at the roots. These ferns had been planted everywhere, as they were maintained by the groundskeepers, and I was concerned about being able to find this spot again. The last thing I wanted to do was to force the rest of Pointe Patrol to haul water buckets all the way back here and lose track of where I was taking them.

I looked around and found a public poop bag dispenser mounted in a nearby area. This was intended as a convenience for the dog owners in the apartments who take their dogs out back to do their business. I grabbed four or five bags and began to use them to mark the hot spot areas I would find.

I went back to the garden area and tied one of the bags around the tallest of the plants in the area. As long as I knew to look for that poop bag, it would be easy to find this spot again.

I then continued around the back of the second-to-last apartment building and made my way down toward the street via the walkway between this and the next building over. The parking lot on this side was farther down Altruria than the entrance to Viewpointe Circle, so I had traveled a long way in my search.

I stopped, halfway down a flight of stairs on the walkway, sensing that a hot spot was near. After finding a few, they got pretty easy to locate. They have their own special smell. By the end of the night, I was pretty much able to just walk right up to them, especially the big ones. I looked over and spotted a huge glowing area next to the last of the buildings in the complex.

Ducking under the handrail by the stairs, I jumped over a man-made decorative creek and then scrambled up a hill to get to where I had seen the embers winking at me. Like the first spot we had found, these embers completely surrounded a tall bush, and the bush reached up just underneath an overhang in the building.

It was the exact same situation as before. If the bush burned, it could catch the overhang, and then the fire would have an easy path all the way from the mulch to the structure. All it needed for that to happen was time and a little wind. Not all hot spots are threatening ones. This one was.

I went back to the railing and tied a bag around it at the same level as the bush. I then went down the stairs to the bottom and tied another bag around the railing there so I could spot it from the street. This particular building had garages on the lower level on the front side, and I took note of the number on the nearest garage door.

Rather than texting, I called Wayne. He answered and sounded exhausted.

"I've got two more spots. One's a bad one," I said, then informed him of my location, all the way at the other end of the apartment complex from where we started.

"OK. Give us a minute, and we'll be there."

I waited a few minutes, then started walking back along the front of the apartments, which was pretty much one giant parking lot. I met the group heading my way about at the halfway mark. They didn't look so good.

Wayne seemed more worn out than usual, and his younger friend, Chip, who had been very energetic and outspoken earlier in the night, was quiet now. It was past 3 a.m.

I noticed that Eddie was completely soaking wet and looked like he was freezing cold. I heard later that he had loosened one of the nuts too far, and the water pressure from the spigot had blown it right off the end of the threads. Water had shot out in a twenty-foot arc over Eddie's head.

Eddie had found the nut, forced it back onto the spigot, and tightened it down by pure force of will. No one had thought he'd be able to do it, but he had surprised them. Unfortunately, the water had sprayed in all directions the whole time he was trying to tighten the nut back on, and his clothes had been completely soaked through. For the rest of the night, he had worked in wet clothes, and it was starting to take a toll on him. If he kept going, he'd probably regret it. He made the wise decision to avoid getting hypothermia and went home to warm up.

The rest of us headed down toward the stairs with the bag tied on the railing, and I pointed out the bad area by the bush. I also mentioned the garden area in the back.

"I'm empty. We've got to stop after this," Wayne said. He and Chip had to get up at 5 a.m. for a long shift the next day. They were due to get about an hour and a half of sleep tonight. The rest of us agreed. We were all running on fumes.

Half the team worked on the embers around the bush, and the rest of us went to deal with the garden area. Fountainview Mike had brought his car around, and we carried water jugs up the stairs and through people's backyards over to the spot I had found earlier that night. We were able to put out half the fire on our first trip, and then had to go back to refill the water jugs.

Sebastian had rigged the hose up on a spigot near the middle of the walkway and filled our bottles up as we waited. I made eye contact with

Wayne, and he smiled and said, "You know they're looting the shit out of our neighborhood right now." We all laughed. Dealing with the Boulders had been hard. We had been out here for hours.

After the second trip to the area in the back, the embers were finally extinguished, and we gathered our equipment and loaded up what we could into Mike's car. He offered to give me a ride back up to the top where I had left my SUV, and I happily accepted.

As we were loading up, we looked across the street and saw a bobbing headlamp. It was almost directly across from us and made its way up the hill toward Viewpointe.

"Is that someone running?" Wayne asked, and we all became alert. Before I knew it, Wayne and Chip were sprinting back toward Viewpointe, their fatigue temporarily forgotten. If that was a looter running from us, they were going to chase him down.

Mike and I followed just behind them in the car. I rolled my window down and unbuckled my seat belt, ready to jump out at a moment's notice if they needed help. The light was just ahead and disappeared into Viewpointe. Whoever it was, they had just picked the absolute worst street in Fountaingrove to duck into.

When we made it to the entrance, Dave, Gary, and Eddie were standing together in the street outside the café, looking at us.

"Did you see someone run in here?" Wayne asked. He spoke with an authority and intensity that reminded us all of what he did for a living. "He was wearing a headlamp." Chip took up position near Wayne, scanning the street. They both had their hands on their weapons.

The guys looked at each other, shaking their heads. Then Gary reached down and turned his headlamp off. He had taken it off his head and tied it to his belt, but he'd forgotten to turn the light off. As he walked back to the circle, the light bounced on his hips, and in the dark from across the street it looked like a runner. We all burst out laughing, relieved.

"I'm glad you guys didn't tackle me or something," he said. No one would have wanted to be the looter that Wayne apprehended on this particular night.

Mike drove me up the street and dropped my off at my car, and we said goodbye. I drove home and backed into the driveway. I went inside, took off my gear, and climbed into bed. I didn't have any problem falling asleep this time. I was totally exhausted.

# CHAPTER 10

# Over the Hump

ELLIOT WAS THE first outsider to text to the thread the next morning. He was up early and sent the text at 5:37 a.m.

## #VIEWPOINTE STRONG

**ELLIOT:** How are you all doing?

Wayne responded. He was the only member of Pointe Patrol who wasn't crashed out at that time.

**WAYNE:** Last night into this morning until 3 a.m. the apartments were highly threatened. A 911 call to fire went unanswered. We put out numerous hot spots knowing if they caught we were doomed. Fatigue setting in 🔥 #VIEW-POINTE STRONG

Bonnie was first to reply.

**BONNIE:** Again if you can reach out to us when something like that happens we can be a phone tree for you, that's the idea we're here to make those calls as you guys take care of business

I don't think Bonnie understood that the fire truck had been reported to us as being on the way but just never showed up. The problem was that the county still had too many fires burning and not enough firefighters to handle each one. As a result, crews were sent to where they could make the most difference, especially if it meant saving lives. Our area, which was supposed to be evacuated, was pretty low on the totem pole because of that. People were more valuable than property. We all ultimately agreed with that approach, even if it had meant we were on our own with regard to fires in the neighborhood.

I think Bonnie regretted the tone of her last text and quickly added another.

> **BONNIE:** I can't believe how grateful we are for everything you guys are doing
>
> **ELLIOT:** Understood hang in there, it's almost daybreak.
>
> **BONNIE:** Please stay safe as I know tired makes it harder 🙏💙

The next messages came in at 7 a.m., when other neighbors in the outside group began to get up.

> **MIKE:** How's everyone doing this morning
>
> **TED:** Just found out 12 hours ago, another 900 firefighters have arrived in Sonoma and Napa. They brought with them 190 engines and 22 dozers!

I was thrilled to read that comment when I woke up and scrolled through the thread later that morning.

> **NICOLE:** I think everyone might have went in for a nap after a long night of patrol/putting out ember fires. Thanks to our Viewpointe heroes, the hood survived another night. 🙏

**SHERI:** Pointe Patrol, you are amazing! I cannot even find the words to describe how grateful we are for you putting yourselves out there, working so hard nonstop, fighting for us to keep our neighborhood, giving us hope, and having our backs when it appears that there is either no one or sparse resources and staff. You have the very minimum, yet you have found a way to maximize it and make it work. You truly are heroes. Thank you. Stay strong—Viewpointe strong—and safe 🙏

Eddie was the first one to get up and respond to the thread, which triggered another batch of grateful replies from the outside group.

**EDDIE:** Good morning! All is good in the hood.

**RHONDA:** Thank you for all the updates. You all are amazing. Keeping you in our thoughts. Stay safe everyone

**DENISE:** Good Morning Pointe Patrol! Thank you Thank you—with love and gratitude 💚🙏

I hadn't seen any of these texts until I woke up around 9 a.m. After spending the night busting our asses, waking up to find that much love directed our way on the thread was a great feeling.

**ME:** Thanks, gang. I think our little group might have kept the apartment complex from burning down last night. 😵 I'm never putting mulch in my yard now

Laura and I got dressed and headed out to the café. Oscar came, too, and hung out on the small patio in front of Eddie's front door while the rest of Pointe Patrol sat at the tables in the driveway having coffee. We didn't just let Oscar lounge by himself up there—one of us always had his leash. The guys greeted him when they saw him, and TJ in particular got a kick out of having Oscar around.

"Should we make breakfast?" I suggested to Eddie after a few minutes of sitting in the sun. I'm the default breakfast chef at our house, so once I'm up I automatically start thinking about what to cook. After the night we all had, a big breakfast sounded awesome to everyone.

"Yeah, let's do it," Eddie agreed, and we started scrounging for supplies. Laura and I had a bunch of stuff that we brought over: eggs, bread, jam, and a brand-new carton of orange juice that we got just before the fire. Other people contributed bagels, a couple sausages, and more eggs. Eddie put on his apron and worked the grill, using a giant frying pan. We had to be careful with toasting bread directly on the surface of the grill, as it was easy to burn it, but no one really cared in the moment.

We found ourselves transported to a different dimension. Society as we had known it faded away. There was no thought of money or personal property. Whatever resources any of us had were freely offered to the group, and everyone's needs were easily met.

The society that we live in during normal times tends to separate people from each other. Everyone lives in their own isolated little box and runs off to do work in other isolating boxes. People don't really connect and tend to live lives that are very apart from any real sense of community. But here, all of those walls were suddenly gone, and Pointe Patrol found that it had become a tribe.

Anthropologists tell us that modern humans have been roaming this planet for over 100,000 years. The vast majority of that time has been spent living in small tribes out in nature, not isolated in cubicles and behind television sets. This is how we as a species have evolved through the ages. We're social creatures. It's in our DNA. Something felt very right about being together like we were. Everyone felt it, and we would have conversations about how different, and yet how strangely wonderful it was to find ourselves living together in this way.

Modern society provides a lot of comfort and safety to its members, no doubt. But with all these advancements, we've lost something important. I never knew it until I got a chance to live in a different way, under a different set of rules. Looking back after the fact, I still wouldn't want to give up my hot showers and internet access to live a more primitive life, but I'd be lying if I said that I didn't miss those connections and the comradery that goes along with it. It's a steep price to have to pay.

The fires were tragic, and many people lost their homes. Some lost their lives or their loved ones. I know this and don't want to be disrespectful. But at the same time, in the middle of all of that loss and destruction, I found myself in a strange sort of paradise. It's funny to call it that, but I don't know a better word. There was just an immense feeling of satisfaction and contentment in living that way, dedicating myself to the well-being and benefit of others.

Now I see why people feel the urge to give up all their belongings and join a commune. They are trying to reconnect with that part of human existence that has been lost in the modern world. For a couple brief weeks, we had that at Pointe Patrol.

Ted texted over the thread.

## #VIEWPOINTE STRONG

**TED:** We're at Safeway—who needs what?

**TED:** Send specs on needs...

Ted and Bonnie were doing a supply run for us. We all sat around, eating our breakfast, and called out items to Fountainview Mike, who reported back to them.

**FOUNTAINVIEW MIKE:** Standing with the group. The main request is coffee beans. They also want eggs. Bread. Food for sandwiches like sandwich meats. Anything you can think of like granola bars or protein bars so people can eat.

**FOUNTAINVIEW MIKE:** Cereal and milk. We're going to hook the generator to the refrigerator so we can keep things cold

We had lots of good ideas for the shopping list, and Mike was furiously texting as we called everything out to him.

**FOUNTAINVIEW MIKE:** Peanut butter and jelly

**FOUNTAINVIEW MIKE:** The group says we're paying for this one

We offered to pay, but there was no chance that the outside group was going to let us pay for anything. When it came to supplies, they had our backs. Big time.

> **FOUNTAINVIEW MIKE:** Maybe hamburgers and hot dogs and buns for dinner. Maybe spaghetti noodles pasta sauce

> **FOUNTAINVIEW MIKE:** Gas for generator if you are able to

For the next hour or so, the conversation on the thread was taken up with logistics. Supplies were being purchased, and various neighbors on the outside were making sure that they got everything we asked for. The big concern was how to get all of it up to us. Not only had there been a large police presence inside the neighborhood in the night, there was a large presence outside of it as well.

Bonnie tried driving up to the Baldwin entrance but had been turned away. The police stationed guards at every street they could find and weren't letting people drive up anymore. She texted us an update.

> **BONNIE:** Hey kids just giving you a heads up there is no way to get a car in here any longer they have every single fire road completely blocked off the only thing you can do is walk in and they're saying you don't even want to do that

Bonnie turned around and tried to give the items to Wayne to take up, but he was completely swamped looking for missing people and wasn't able to take any time out of his schedule. Instead, she and Ted had found a sheriff's deputy who was willing to help. I don't know if they knew him already, made friends with him on the spot, or if he was a friend of Wayne's. But in any case, he had our supplies now and was going to deliver them.

> **BONNIE:** Hi guys we need somebody at the coffee shop. To wait for the sheriff's officer who is bringing up the food and gas. You need to be there to meet him he's getting ready to leave the sheriff station now

Ted rephrased.

> **TED:** Food on the way up via Sheriff Dept

We were waiting at the café when the police car pulled up. The deputy came out and handed us bags stuffed full of groceries and two full gas containers. He was very friendly and was glad to help. Not only had the police been guarding our neighborhood and keeping it safe at night, now they were bringing us groceries! Like our own neighborhood, but on a much larger scale, Sonoma County had been pulling together in the face of the fires, and that included the police.

Soon after the deputy made his delivery, Bonnie sent over some good news.

> **BONNIE:** Hey everyone because there's a couple of people on this list that are not in the circle locally. I just wanted to let everybody know that we have been assigned a firetruck to the area to watch for fires. And our amazing Pointe Patrol can get some rest. And we can breathe a little easier. Each day a little step further away from real danger.
>
> **WAYNE:** Amen 🙏
>
> **MIKE:** That is amazing!
>
> **NORMA:** Woo Hoo!

It was great news. Having a fire truck just for our neighborhood would be a major improvement. It would be especially critical if we ended up coming across another situation like the one we stumbled into last night at the Boulders.

Earlier in the day, Wayne had run across another group of neighbors that had stuck around to protect their houses. This group was from the small cul-de-sac street just above the Boulders, across the street from Gardenview Circle. He sent the information to us over the Pointe Patrol thread.

### Pointe Patrol

> **WAYNE:** Let's make sure to get with that crew above us, they are dialed and have resources for us like gas... good redneck folks, salt-of-the-earth types. They have pull to sneak stuff in also, I think like 2 cops up there

**SEBASTIAN:** Ok, we're headed up there

**WAYNE:** SMART move I think

Sebastian and two other guys got together and headed up Altruria to make contact with the other group. This made a lot of sense for a couple of reasons. First, if one of the groups needed help in an emergency flare-up situation, having other people able and willing to assist just a couple minutes away could be the difference between saving a neighborhood and losing one. Second, if both groups were aggressively patrolling for looters (and potentially armed), we needed to make friends and become acquainted with each other. It was important to know what the other good guys looked like.

Twenty minutes after the three had headed up the hill, I saw a text come in from Sebastian. They had successfully made contact.

**SEBASTIAN:** Got in touch, they have our info and will coordinate on the boulders. They are planning to get a 200' hose and water pump if needed.

**WAYNE:** SICK!!! You rock

For lunch, we ate chips and sandwiches. We had broken into our new groceries and found that our shoppers had overlooked nothing. TJ put avocado on his, then spent a good five minutes extolling the virtues of putting a fried egg on hamburger. The conversation was lighthearted, and we were all in a good mood.

We had come to the unanimous agreement that the Boulders apartment complex had been misnamed. From this point forward, we decided that it would be far more fitting and appropriate to call it *The Smolders*. Many of us had seen enough last night to forever swear off using mulch in our yards, myself included.

I was sitting across from Dave and took the opportunity to ask him about how the fire had first made it to the neighborhood during the time when he was here alone.

"I first watched the fire come over the hill, behind the apartments," he began. "It happened after the sun was up, so it was already light, and

I could see everything. As the hill burned, the flames began forming into what looked like little spinning tornados of fire. Each of those stretched up a hundred feet into the air, and they shot embers out their tops.

"I call it 'fire from the sky.' Hundreds of these embers came down on the neighborhood. They were all red hot, and some of them were as big around as a dinner plate."

This explained some of what I had found in my front yard. Until then, I couldn't understand how those huge black coals had found their way onto my otherwise perfectly green lawn.

"The embers would land on roofs and next to houses. One of them landed in the dry brush on the hill below the house on the corner. That's how it went down. That's how Miramonte started, too. I watched that neighborhood go up house by house, one right after the other.

"I was busting my ass running around putting out those embers. They were everywhere. At that time, the hoses weren't working. There was too big of a drain on the water from other emergency crews, and we lost all our water pressure. I had to use water from my hot tub.

"But I'm old. I can't carry five-gallon buckets of water around like I used to. So I would only fill them up halfway instead, and that's how I put out most of the fires early on."

He then continued and retold us the story of how he had dealt with the fire at Ted and Cathy's house, eventually putting out their bed with a garden hose.

"The heat was intense. I was there with a T-shirt, and it was almost unbearable. Back when I worked for San Francisco Fire, we'd have to go into burning houses all the time, so I'm used to being around fire. But back then I had gear to protect me from the heat.

"A lot of fire crews like to spray water on fire from a long distance and don't actually go into burning buildings. It's safer that way, because you can keep your distance. But you can't do it like that in San Francisco, where all the walls are shared. You'll lose the whole city if you just try to spray water from the outside. The only way to put out the fire is to go inside, find it, and knock it down at the source.

"A company is usually made up of five engines, and one of those is the big one with the ladder like you see in movies. What they do is get to the top of the building and cut a hole in the roof. That gives the smoke a way to escape, so that the other teams can see when they go inside.

"A lot of times you don't know what you're walking into. You just go in and blindly feel your way toward the fire. Not all firefighters do it that way. But that's how we did it."

We were all listening now. I don't know how many of us knew what Dave had done when he was younger. I certainly hadn't. Until the fire, he was just the nice retired guy that was always very friendly at our neighborhood potlucks. I never knew he was a badass firefighter who used to run into burning buildings.

"There's one thing I have to say. I was in the Oakland Hills Fire, so I've seen this before. But here, every time we came to a point when the neighborhood could have burned, something saved us. If Martha's house caught at the same time as I was at Ted's, we would have burned. Had I not found the fire company when I did, we would have burned. Had the second engine come even a minute later than it did, we would have burned. In this fire, things happened just when they needed to happen. Over and over. Had things happened any other way than they did, we would have lost the neighborhood. We were lucky, but it was more than that. I've never seen anything like it."

"It was the hand of God," I said.

"Yes." Dave and I looked at each other, feeling immense gratitude.

"By the way, about that reporter that was here the other day," he said, changing the subject. "If they come back, I want you to know I'm not going to speak to them. If you send them to me, I'm just going to close the door right in their face. I don't have anything to say.

"I didn't save the neighborhood. I might have been here first, but we've all saved the neighborhood countless times since then. Each one of you has done something that saved the neighborhood since you've been here. In over three decades of doing this, it was never about one person. It has always been about the team.

"I won't be singled out. I don't want you telling reporters that 'Dave' did anything. Don't even use my name."

"What should we call you then? Should we change your name?" someone asked.

Laura suggested that we refer to Dave as *Clave*, which Dave laughed at when she used it. Eddie called him *Steve* a number of times, picking the name randomly out of the air. But in the end, if he didn't want to be called Dave, we thought the best alternate name would be *Chief*. Dave seemed to like that, and it described his role among us very well. From that point forth, that's how we referred to him, and still do sometimes.

We kept up our regular patrols during the day, but there wasn't much work to do as far as putting out fires or hot spots. All of the bad ones had been dealt with last night. So for the most part, everyone just took lots of walks around the neighborhood, obsessively double-checking to make sure it was all still there. Police and fire trucks routinely visited and would do slow laps around the circle. Everyone smiled and waved whenever we saw them.

One of the tasks I hadn't been looking forward to doing, but knew was necessary, was to figure out how to take a shower. It had been a couple days, and I was getting ripe. Taking a cold shower is no fun, but it was the only option. I became quite proficient at it over the next few days.

Obviously, it's the *cold* part of *cold shower* that is the problem. Standing under freezing water while naked is just not something that anyone really enjoys doing. So the key is to find ways to minimize the discomfort. That means taking the shower during the hottest part of the day, so you can go out in the sun afterward and warm up. The other thing that helps is to wash each body part separately, rather than all at once. So I would get into the shower, but only stand at the edge of the water. Then I'd do an arm, and then a leg, and then my head—each body part in its own turn. As long as I took it in stages like that, it wasn't nearly as shocking as if I tried plunging my entire body in like I did with a hot shower. There was still the issue of getting my back and chest clean, which was more intense, but for the most part I found that it wasn't that bad of an experience.

After my shower, I went out and took Oscar for one of his hourly patrols. As we passed the café, TJ spotted Oscar and shouted out to him.

"Hey, Oscar!"

Oscar had been getting used to the group and was warming up to them. I didn't let him run freely among them as I would have had he been a Golden Retriever, but I could tell that he knew who they were and that he didn't consider them strangers anymore. Everyone except Sebastian, that is. For whatever reason, Oscar liked to bark at Sebastian.

I had long abandoned wearing my mask. It was just too cumbersome and suffocating. I preferred to be able to breathe, even though it meant I'd be constantly breathing what smelled like campfire. The rest of Pointe Patrol had done the same. The side effect of that decision was that a lot of us were always coughing and hacking. I had a low-level sore throat that was just part of the experience of being in the neighborhood. That sore throat lasted for months.

Laura, in particular, was really being troubled by the smoke. It was especially irritating to her at night when she was trying to sleep. The smoke smell even came up off the pillows and blankets. I remember seeing particles of ash fly up in the air the first night when I put my head down on a pillow. Everything in the house was covered in a layer of soot, even though our windows had been closed during the fire.

Laura had contacted her doctor about the issue, and they had prescribed a special inhaler to help her. The problem was that in order to get the inhaler, someone needed to drive to the pharmacy in Rohnert Park, the next city south of Santa Rosa along 101. Kaiser here had been closed down, and the hospital had been evacuated due to the fires.

Since we were locked in, the task fell to the outside group, and Joe and Carmen were more than happy to volunteer. They had evacuated to a home in Monte Rio, about thirty minutes away, and during the day they would try to do whatever odd jobs were required on the outside, such as grocery runs, pharmacy runs, or even standing in line to try to get mail. Today, they found themselves driving down to Rohnert Park for Laura's inhaler.

When they got to Kaiser, Carmen texted the thread.

## #VIEWPOINTE STRONG

**CARMEN:** Laura, I'm here, but need your medical record number. 😊

I texted the number over to her privately once I saw her note come through. Pretty soon, she and Joe were at the Baldwin gate, waiting on the other side of the police line.

I jumped in my car and drove down to meet them, parking on the other side of the police car that was pulled across the Baldwin fire gate. The police officer there was friendly but wasn't letting anyone past. He was wearing a bulletproof vest and was ready for the worst, should it happen.

The law is that no one can force you to leave your house, even if you live in an evacuation zone. However, once you're out, they most definitely can force you to stay out. Because of that, there was a big difference in what you could do depending on which side of the barrier you were on.

I greeted the officer, asked him how things were going, and made some chit chat about fires and looters. It was a boring job, sitting there all day, and I always made a point to try to engage whomever I met that was guarding the neighborhood. They were people, too, despite the uniforms, and they always seemed very friendly and open as long as I approached them in the same way.

Joe had brought a bunch of heavy bags of ice for us, and when the officer saw him open up his trunk and start to lift one, he went over and helped. He was a young guy and could easily carry three or four bags at once. As the police officer loaded the back of my car up with ice, I gave both Joe and Carmen a hug, thanking them. They passed over the white bag from Kaiser and a few other things.

I said my goodbyes, waved to the officer, and headed back up the hill to deliver the supplies. The café had plenty of ice chests, thanks to Gary, and now we could completely fill them all with ice. Between that and the fridge, we were set as far as food and beverage storage went.

When I had given Laura her inhaler, she texted Joe and Carmen on the small group chat that the four of us shared.

### Joe, Carmen, Laura, and Earik

**LAURA:** Earik just returned with the goods. I'm sorry you had to go through so much to get it here! I really, really appreciate it!

**CARMEN:** Noooo apologies necessary. It's all about "we are a team." Thank YOU for all you're doing for all of us. Please take care, and get some rest if you can now. 🖤

**ME:** I'm sleeping the whole night tonight! Not having to do night patrols anymore is such a relief

**JOE:** You earned it!!!

**JOE:** 😪

Laura got lucky. Kaiser soon ran out of their supply of those inhalers and had trouble getting more. The air quality was terrible. They had it even worse in Napa, where the air quality ranked as the absolute worst in the nation due to the high levels of particulates and ozone. It was up to the "hazardous" level, the most dangerous on the Environmental Protection Agency's scale.

Now that we had police and fire trucks doing regular patrols through the neighborhood, our jobs became a lot less demanding. The focus shifted more to cleaning up and managing the neighborhood, rather than preventing it from burning down.

We all took the opportunity to put up our flags, and everyone who had one available hung it out.

## #VIEWPOINTE STRONG

**LAURA:** Please hang your American flag if you have one #VIEWPOINTE PROUD 🇺🇸🇺🇸🇺🇸

**TED:** Feel free to fly mine!

**NORMA:** 🇺🇸🇺🇸🇺🇸🇺🇸🇺🇸 #ViewpointeStrong 🇺🇸🇺🇸🇺🇸🇺🇸🇺🇸

Finding myself with plenty of light left in the day and some spare time on my hands, I sent out the following text to the thread.

**ME:** Now that the professionals are here and I don't have to patrol around, I spent some time cleaning up the yard. Our potted plants were parched. I'll go around and check on everyone's front yard now, but if you want me to go in your backyard and deal with something, just ask. 😊No need to let the plants die if they don't have to

Normally, I hate doing yard work. But today was different. I liked doing things for the neighbors. It felt good to be useful to others. The requests began to come in.

**TED:** Too much glass on our backyard but the front could use a dousing... thank you!

**ELLIOT:** Thanks Laura, if you could water in our backyard that would be great. You can also take all the figs and kale you like. There is a hose already.

**ME:** Bribing with figs gets you to the front of the line

**ME:** (This is Earik. I'll see if I can recruit Laura, too)

**ELLIOT:** Ha sorry about that. Lol your choice!!!

So Laura and I began to make our way around the neighborhood, watering people's lawns and their plants. Gary saw what we were doing and jumped in to help. Being a hardware guy, he was very familiar with all the various kinds of drip irrigation systems that people had installed and was able to get them to function even though we didn't have power.

Not everyone had a hose in their yard anymore, since we had scavenged a lot of things in the last few days. Because of that, I made sure to take a watering can along with me, which I found myself using quite often.

Two days ago, a deer had taken refuge from the fires in Ted's yard, and Ted and Cathy had been worried about him.

> **TED:** Also a deer was resting in our side yard when we were up there on Tuesday! We put out a big bucket of water in the side yard by the back fence for him. If it's possible to check on that...

The deer wasn't in Ted's yard anymore, but someone had definitely been into the water. There wasn't any left. I refilled the bucket in case any thirsty animals showed up later.

> **JOE:** I watered all mine yesterday. So we should be good. I have an American flag and pole next to the garage door to the house. No need to take down the flag at dusk. You can fly Old Glory 24/7 till we're all back. 😎
>
> **LAURA:** Will do!!! U got watered again anyway

I had thought it would only take a short time to water everyone's yard, but it actually turned out to be quite a task, especially since I didn't want to do a crappy job and have the neighbors come back to dead plants after I had promised to water them. It helped that there were three of us working on it, and we managed to get it all done before dinner.

Wayne brought supplies on his way home.

### Pointe Patrol

> **WAYNE:** What do you need before I head up the hill?
>
> **TJ:** HOT DOGS PLEASE!!
>
> **LAURA:** Like 20

**ME:** Do we have beer?

**LAURA:** I have mustard. We need ketchup

**TJ:** We don't have beer

**WAYNE:** I got beer

**ME:** You rock

**WAYNE:** Okay give me a minute and I'll bring the party. Sorry Dave no disco ball

**WAYNE:** Buns?

**LAURA:** Got buns

**WAYNE:**

And so we had our first big dinner feast, which consisted of hot dogs, chips, and beer. Hot dogs and beer turned out to be pretty much all we seemed to eat over the next week, with only a few exceptions. What became really funny was how much beer we were able to accumulate. For whatever reason, whenever anyone in the outside group wanted to do something nice for us, they would buy us beer and ice. Within days we had so much beer and ice that we couldn't find a place to put it all despite having a full-size refrigerator and three large coolers at our disposal.

After Wayne had returned, and we had eaten, he noticed all the flags that were flying. Being a very patriotic kind of guy, he wasn't going to be left out and went home to get his flag, too. He wanted to hang it across the street from the café but didn't have a pole that would work. Gary did though. Gary had all sorts of stuff in his garage, including extra flag poles.

As he watched Gary successfully raise his flag across from where we were sitting, Wayne took a sip from his beer and said, "You know, I almost drowned trying to get that flag."

"I was up at Tahoe with my little guy, and we were out paddling in a boat. The water was crystal clear, and when we looked down, we saw an American flag at the bottom of the lake.

"'Get it, Daddy!' Hunter told me. So I said 'OK!' and jumped in.

"But it was too far down, and I couldn't reach it. It was so cold. And the pressure was crushing. When I got back up, I knew I was in trouble. But I couldn't let Hunter see me fail. I *had* to get that flag!

"So I tried again and got it the second time. It almost killed me, though."

After dinner, Laura and I said good night to everyone and headed home. Oscar would get another quick walk around the circle at some point, but this wasn't going to be another round-the-clock night of patrols. Now that the police and fire department were in the neighborhood, we could all rest easier, and I was excited at the opportunity of being able to sleep through the night in my own bed. This would be the first time I'd been able to do that since the day before we evacuated.

As I got ready for bed, I took a peek out the bedroom window to see what was going on in Miramonte. It had become somewhat of a habit to check on that neighborhood every time I went to bed. Like yesterday, I could see a police car parked at the entrance. They didn't have all their spotlights on like the previous night, but they were there all the same. We were being guarded.

As we were lying in bed, Laura and I spent some time talking about the day and sharing our impressions on everything that happened. Aside from the smoke smell, it almost felt like a normal night.

I reached over and kissed her, then slid my hand down the side of her body.

"Are you trying to have sex… ?" she asked. She seemed a little surprised.

After she realized that, *yes*, that was exactly what I was trying to do, she added, "Let's do it tomorrow." That was a typical tactic when she was only halfway in the mood and wanted to turn down an advance but not totally slam the door on it. That strategy wouldn't work on me tonight.

"There might not be a tomorrow," I replied. "Look what's happening out there. It's the End of the World."

We made eye contact in the darkness and, without another word, fell into each other's arms, overcome with passion and desire. A long time ago I read an article that said the best kind of movie to take a first date to is an action flick. The writer argued that it was because action movies get your blood pumping and your adrenaline flowing, and that is much more conductive to having a good first date than something intellectual or cute.

These past few days, Laura and I had been more than watching an action movie—we had been living in one. Spending the days putting out fires, confronting looters, and risking our lives to varying degrees grounded us in the moment. Our senses were sharper, and our feelings stronger. Everything was clearer and more vibrant.

That night, together in our bed, on the wrong side of the evacuation line and surrounded by death and destruction, the Universe was suddenly perfect. There was no past and no future. The fire was forgotten, and the neighborhood disappeared. There were no bills, or work, or distractions. We were completely and fully embodied in the present moment, perfectly absorbed in the one other person that we both loved most in the world.

I've never had sex like that before. I didn't think it could actually be that good. It was *by far* the most amazing I've ever experienced, and Laura feels the same way. We still talk about that night from time to time. For us, we refer to what happened as *End of the World Sex*, and that experience has joined a handful of other moments that represent the high points of our relationship.

Honestly, I don't think it would be possible to achieve a transcendental union like that in normal times. It's not easily recreated because it requires a lot of stress and adrenaline to set the stage, and that isn't something that you usually get in regular day-to-day life. If you ever find yourself in a disaster situation and happen to have your lover with you, make sure to do whatever it takes to find some time to be with that person. Sometimes catastrophes can have unexpected silver linings.

# CHAPTER 11

# Return of the Twins
### (Peaches and Squatchie)

AS USUAL, WAYNE was up first the next morning, and being a police officer, he had naturally been thinking about looters. He texted instructions to us through the thread.

**#VIEWPOINTE STRONG**

**WAYNE:** DON'T GET TOO COMFORTABLE

**WAYNE:** for the foreseeable future as with the "Valley Fire" we will have heavy traffic in our area. Lookie Lou, and people posing as insurance, contractors, PG&E, you name it. Some legit and some not. Continue to ask for credentials if it doesn't look right…. Take pictures of them and their vehicle. A legit person would understand that. #VIEWPOINTE STRONG is a special little place ♥ and we look out for one another. Thanks again to everyone for everything. You all fought 🔥 with 🔥
Best,
Wayne

**BONNIE:** thank you Wayne—and everyone up there—LET us know what you need today and we'll try to get more care packages up there.

**EDDIE:** Café is open

**EDDIE:** Coffee is brewing

**TED:** State Farm team has IDs hanging from lanyards around their necks in case you see them

**WAYNE:** So does a good scam artist

**BONNIE:** That photo idea is great—photographing them and their car

**WAYNE:** Confront them you'll know

**BONNIE:** 💪

**WAYNE:** The good ones do their homework, they know names of people living at addresses, etc.

I made my way over to the café, and Laura joined me soon after. I brought Oscar, and I sat on the steps to Eddie and TJ's front door as I drank my coffee.

TJ had always been very enthusiastic whenever Oscar made an appearance, and this morning was no different. He sat at the tables we had arranged in the driveway, watching Oscar and smiling. It was unusual for TJ not to be happy; he had a very outgoing personality.

"Do you want to meet him?" Laura asked after a few minutes.

"Yeah! Can I?" TJ asked, leaping up.

"OK, but you have to do it in a certain way," I said, stopping him from just running over and throwing his arms around Oscar. "You have to let him sniff you first. Hold out the back of your hand to him."

I held mine out to demonstrate. From a dog's perspective, it's rude to just walk right up and start petting them. If you approach head-on, then it's both rude and aggressive. Pet dogs are generally subservient to people and put up with being offended all the time, but working dogs are different. If someone they don't like is rude and insulting to them, they might decide to do something about it. So the correct way to approach a dog is not directly head-on, but a little to the side, and then you stop and let them smell you first. It mimics how other dogs would act in the same situation. You offer the back of your hand in case the dog is grouchy. It's much better to get bit on the back than the underside where all the veins are.

TJ came over and extended his hand to Oscar as instructed. Oscar sniffed him politely, then quickly moved forward, pressing the side of his body up against TJ's legs. Oscar was leaning on TJ, giving him a full body hug.

"Now you're part of the inner circle!" I said, happy that it had gone well.

"Whoa!" TJ exclaimed. Getting a Doberman hug can be a rush, especially if it's a new experience and you're not used to big dogs. Oscar wasn't looking at TJ as he was hugging him but was scanning down the street. He was still on the job.

"Look, he's guarding you," Laura said. Dobermans can be scary looking, and very intimidating to strangers, but once you get on their good side, they're highly protective and overwhelmingly affectionate. I don't know how much time Oscar spends with his head on my leg each day, looking up at me adoringly, but it's not an insignificant amount. Now TJ was going to get some love, too.

Over the next few days, Oscar met most of the group. Dave, Wayne, and Gary all learned how to introduce themselves and made friends with him. Fountainview Mike even had Oscar's head buried in his lap for pets at one point. They had gotten used to him, and he had gotten used to them. I have always been a little overprotective of Oscar, and it was nice to see him become part of the group. It was the first time since he was a puppy that any of our neighbors accepted him for who he was and praised him rather than complained about him.

Laura and I had been in contact with Judith, and it was getting clear that the cats were too much for her. I suspect that they had turned her library into their own personal litter box. It was time for us to get them.

The plan was for Laura to get out to Graton somehow, and then come back with her car and the cats. We both thought she'd be able to get back through the lines as long as I was there to escort her, but in case she didn't, it would just be the animals and me, and Laura would stay on the outside. Now that the fires were pretty much controlled, she had begun to feel the pull to go back to her social work job and help people in the community in that capacity.

She sent a text out to the thread.

> **LAURA:** I need a ride from police line to Graton today. Is that close to anyone's route (I don't need a ride back)

Joe and Carmen responded right away and were up to the task.

> **JOE:** Laura. Carmen and Joe here. We can take you to Graton

> **LAURA:** Awesome. Let me know when you are ready!

Our conversation was mixed in with a lot of other texts in the thread. There was always a flurry of activity during the first part of the day, with people checking in and arranging various tasks. Somehow we needed more ice, probably because our beer-to-ice ratio had become unbalanced toward the beer side of the equation. Joe and Carmen volunteered to get some for us on their way up.

> **JOE:** I'll bring some ice for you when we pick up Laura. I'll text when close.

> **BONNIE:** If someone could grab one or two bags of ice for Dave that would be awesome. Thank you

Twenty minutes later, Joe sent an update to us.

> **JOE:** I have 100lbs of ice to give to Earik when we get there. 30 minutes

As we waited, a text came through from Wayne. He had been working missing persons cases.

> **WAYNE:** Has anyone heard from Elaine? She is reported missing

**BONNIE:** No, she is not missing, she is with Edward and Helga out in Monte Rio. She is fine and healthy

The one regret I had about the night we evacuated was that we hadn't pounded on Elaine's door to check on her. She had actually left an hour before we had, but we didn't know that at the time. We had already double-checked to make sure that she was OK when we had reconnected with the rest of the neighbors.

As I took Oscar around the circle for a patrol, I stopped at the burned-out house on the corner. It was a frequent stopping place. Since it was up on the hill, it provided a great view of Miramonte below. Today, there was a swarm of blue PG&E utility trucks down there.

I looked more closely and realized that PG&E had sent one truck for every house in the neighborhood. They were making sure the gas lines were all capped and turned off, so that when gas returned to the neighborhood, nothing would accidentally light up again down there.

I snapped a picture and sent it over to the thread. I was impressed.

**ME:** Not sure if the pic shows it, but there's a PGE truck on every house in Miramonte

**EDDIE:** PGE are shutting down the gas on every home up here.

**DOTTIE:** Was it still on?

**SEBASTIAN:** No, but they have to cap every gas line that broke and close gas for all the homes

**SEBASTIAN:** After they do that, they will open the main, then come open each house which was not damaged

**DOTTIE:** Thanks

**BONNIE:** Got it, bless their hearts for being out there working on it

A couple minutes later, Joe had arrived at the gate.

**JOE:** Earik, Carmen and I are here at Baldwin. Here for Laura too.

Laura and I loaded up and drove down to the Baldwin gate. There was a different police officer stationed there this time.

I went out and greeted him, telling him what we were all doing. He didn't have a problem with it, and we spent a few minutes chatting. I always liked to ask whomever was stationed there if they had been in any adventures.

"Do you get any looters trying to sneak through here?" I asked.

He laughed. "Oh, yeah. We're constantly turning people away. There's a never-ending stream of them trying to talk their way in."

I loaded up the ton of ice that Joe had brought, and then Laura crossed the line and drove off with Joe and Carmen. I watched them go, then waved goodbye to the police officer and headed back up to the circle.

I texted an update about what I had learned to Pointe Patrol.

### Pointe Patrol

**ME:** Talked to a cop down at the gate. He says the current looter strategy is fake press badges. FYI

**WAYNE:** To put simply, these turds 💩 sit in jail for hundreds of days per year or state prison for years at a time and think of all the scams. Question everybody and then have follow-up questions.

**ME:** 💩💩💩

**EDDIE:** These A-holes can't touch us. VS for life!

After I got back and had done a round with Oscar, I made my way over to the café. We had been running low on our own bottled water, and I needed to replenish the supply. Finding drinking water wasn't a problem though—there was tons of it in the café and in front of Wayne's house. It was just a matter of helping yourself to what you needed.

Gary and I stopped to talk, and Dave approached us. He was concerned about rotten food in people's refrigerators. Not everyone had been able to empty their refrigerators, and the longer the food sat like that, the worse it would get. People had been giving their house keys to Bonnie, and she'd pass them forward during various supply runs. All of those keys ended up finding their way to Dave, who had become the Key Master. He had a Tupperware container filled with them, each tagged with a piece of masking tape with the address written on it.

It was time to empty all that old food out of people's refrigerators, and he needed some help. Gary and I certainly didn't want to let Dave do that kind of a job alone, so we jumped in to assist.

Equipped with some big black garbage bags, Gary and I began to work. What made things difficult is that Dave didn't want to let more than one key out of his possession at a time. I don't know if it was because he felt responsible for people's houses since he was the Key Master, or if he didn't totally trust us, or if he was just a bit of a control freak, but getting keys from him was like pulling teeth.

The refrigerators all stunk, but some were worse than others. Martha had the easiest one to deal with by far. She was a vegetarian and only had a few things. On the other end of the spectrum, some people had their fridges jam-packed with food that had already started to go bad before the fire, and I had to hold my breath when dealing with those. Most fridges were one-bag jobs, but there were definitely exceptions.

Once I'd thrown away all the perishable items, I'd clean up any messes from things that had melted or leaked in the freezer. That part wasn't any fun. When I was done, I'd tie off the bag and haul it out to the trash can. I was surprised at how heavy some of those bags were! The refrigerator doors were left propped open, so that they could air out.

We didn't know when garbage pickup might resume, but rotten food was better off sitting outside than stinking up the house. The only houses we didn't clean up were ones that we didn't have keys to, or ones that had already been dealt with by their owners. We wondered if we should do the house down the Q with the kicked-in door, but didn't have explicit permission, so decided to steer clear. We weren't going into anyone's house uninvited, rotten food or not.

After all the fridges had been cleaned out, and I had taken a break for lunch, a text came through from Denise. She lived in the house where the tree limb had come down on the BMW.

## #VIEWPOINTE STRONG

**DENISE:** Hi! This is Denise—just now reading text I have no cell at work. Is there any way I can catch a ride in to turn off my alarm if still going and empty fridge? Or a way I can get my key to someone?

**ME:** Go to the Baldwin gate and I can drive you up from that side.

**DENISE:** When is good for you?

**ME:** Earik's shuttle service is operational 24/7 at this point. 😜

A few minutes later, in between a bunch of other side texts, Helene chimed in about the Baldwin gate.

**HELENE:** Baldwin gate had police stay over there this morning when i was trying to walk through the police did not let me

**ME:** If you have one of us meet you on the other side it's easier to get through. Too many scammers pretending to need to get through

**DENISE:** Is now better or 3:30 ok?

**ME:** Now better

**DENISE:** I will be there in 5 min!!!

I got in my car and started to head out. Eddie was standing in the street, and I slowed as he flagged me down.

"Want some company?" he asked.

"Sure, jump in!"

We drove down to the gate together, commenting on the burned houses we passed along the way. It had already been four days since the fire, but it would take longer than that to get used to these kinds of changes in the neighborhood.

We beat Denise to the gate, got out, and started talking to the police. Eddie pulled out his phone and began showing them videos he had recorded on the first day. He had been through Coffey Park early, which was a scene of otherworldly devastation at that time. I had already seen the video once—it was intense, to say the least.

I stepped back as I felt a text come through and vibrate my phone.

**DENISE:** This is Denise. I am here!

**DENISE:** Who will be here? They want your name.

Denise was at the wrong gate.

**ME:** I'm here too. Which entrance are you at?

**DENISE:** I'm off Terra Linda at Lake Park

Denise was at the other gate, farther down Lake Park.

**ME:** I'll come down.

Eddie and I hopped back in the car to drive over to the other gate. The gate was closed, and there was an officer standing on our side of it. Denise was on the other side, along with a crowd of half a dozen other people, all trying to talk their way in.

Eddie and I approached the officer and greeted him. Eddie took the lead.

"Hi. We're here from Viewpointe Circle, up the hill. This is our neighbor. She just wants to come up and clean out her fridge. We can drive her up," Eddie explained.

The cop was having none of it. He was not in a good mood.

"Nobody crosses the line," he said, matter-of-factly, in a flat tone.

Up until this point, all of the police I had interacted with had been on my side. That even went for the six that had surrounded me a couple nights ago. This felt a lot different. This guy wasn't on our side at all. Eddie began to try to talk to him more, trying to explain our situation and who we were, and to vouch for Denise in that way. I moved away, toward where Denise stood on the other side of the gate.

I said "Hi" to her, and then spoke to her as quietly as I was able, without making it look like we were being sneaky. "If this doesn't work, go down the hill and take the first left before you get to the main road. I'll meet you at that gate."

She nodded in understanding, and then we made small talk as Eddie kept working on the officer.

"She's not coming through this line," I heard the officer say with finality. That was it. He wasn't going to budge.

We stopped pushing, then thanked him for guarding the neighborhood, and said goodbye to Denise. She waved back, and we all drove off.

"That guy was not going to let anyone through," Eddie said, as we drove over to the Baldwin gate. "He said something like, 'I'm the only person doing my job up here.'"

"You'd think he'd have some understanding, though. She's not a looter. She's just going to clean out her fridge. We're here to vouch for her and be her escorts," I said.

"He might not want to be here. He might have lost his house in the fire, and now he has to deal with all of us."

We pulled up to the Baldwin gate and greeted the police officers again. Denise had just pulled up, too. We explained that we just wanted to take her up, and then would bring her right back in an hour. They were fine with it and let her through.

We drove back up, and I went slow so Denise could take in the neighborhood for the first time. It was one thing to know houses had burned down, it was another to see the ruins with your own two eyes.

I dropped everyone off back at Viewpointe and told Denise to let me know when she needed a ride back. Eddie and I had put a tarp over her car earlier that morning, and she was very grateful to all of us for taking care of her house. She wanted to go through and check everything inside, then planned to leave a key with Dave before she left in case one of us needed to take care of something for her later.

I texted the thread with an update. I was concerned that we were going to overwhelm the police and force them to take more of a hardline stance on us. The grouchy police officer had made an impression.

> **ME:** OK. This may not work for long. Not all cops are cool with people coming through. If it's not critical, better to let us manage things for you. Deliver a key to us through the line rather than try to get driven up. That way we can keep the cops from getting in trouble

> **WAYNE:** Yes, it's getting ridiculous with everyone being a special snowflake... that said figure shit out with the group and prioritize what it is you really need. Consolidate and give me one or two requests for the day PLEASE!

It was obvious the neighbors had been trying to take advantage of Wayne's position as a police officer, and he probably had gotten in trouble for being too accommodating to them.

> **BONNIE:** Thank you Wayne for going above and beyond. We can absolutely get our act together and I think we need to focus on things like getting supplies to you guys. And any medications that we have in our house. But at the end of the day that should be it

Mike sent over a picture of a computer screen, showing a post on the Facebook page of the Sonoma County Sheriff's Office. A lady named Linda had posted the following:

A nice young man pounded on our door in Fountaingrove (Viewpointe Circle) to inform us we will soon need to evacuate. Out of fear that a stranger is pounding on our door in the wee hours of the morning, we didn't open our door. Thanks to this fine man, who said he works for the sheriff's office, who had the mind set to return to pound on our door a second time, I cannot thank him enough for saving our lives. I need to know who he is, so I can personally thank him. We were at the very end of the private lane off Viewpointe Circle and lost our home. Will someone please help me find my angel and tell me how I can thank him? Until then, I'll call him Angel Gabriel. Thank you to all who put their lives on the line for residents and total strangers. I'm breathing because of you all.

Now I knew who had lived at the far end of the *Q*. Her name was Linda. Wayne was the guardian angel she was trying to thank.

I heard back from Laura. She had made it to Judith's and was driving back with Peaches and Squatchie. She'd be at the gate soon.

Norma also sent a text. She had been baking brownies for Pointe Patrol all morning and was ready to deliver them to us across the police line.

> **NORMA:** Earik—I am about 5 minutes away. Can you meet me at the bottom of Baldwin to receive the brownies? Norma
>
> **ME:** Heading down now. Will wait for you there
>
> **ME:** Offer a brownie to the peaches Luce down there. They've been helpful with this stuff when they didn't have to be
>
> **ME:** Police. Not peaches. Peaches is my cat

I let Denise know I was ready to head back down and found that she was ready to leave as well. The timing had worked out, and I'd be able to handle three jobs in one trip.

We drove out and soon found ourselves back at the Baldwin gate. Norma was waiting on the other side.

Everyone greeted the police, and I was glad to see that it was the same friendly ones who had been here earlier. Denise crossed back over the line, waving to Norma as she passed by on the way to her parked car. Norma came up and presented me with a tray of brownies for Pointe Patrol, which were amazing. I didn't expect those to last long.

Laura pulled up just as I was putting the brownies in my car. She and Norma hugged, and we all chatted together for a few minutes. The police remembered Laura from earlier in the day and knew all about her mission to bring the cats home.

I expected that I'd be able to get the cats across the line, but I hoped that the police would be fine with Laura coming back as well. What I didn't expect was them to be fine letting her drive her car back up, but that's what they did, pulling up the posts to clear the way for her. Sometimes there are big benefits to being extra friendly and courteous to the police.

When Laura and I made it back to the circle, she parked in our driveway, and I parked next door at Dottie's. Dottie's house is visible from the entrance to the circle, and I thought it would be better for looters to see cars in both driveways rather than just one. We made sure to back in should we need to make a hasty evacuation later.

Peaches and Squatchie seemed glad to be home. They had been living in one room for days now and clearly appreciated being let out. They wanted us to let them run around outside, but that wasn't going to happen. As long as the threat of having to escape from a fire still loomed, we were going to keep the cats close so we could take them with us.

"Sorry, guys, you're going to be indoor cats for a while," Laura told them, as they looked out the windows longingly.

Bonnie texted the thread with a new proposal for how to manage interactions between Pointe Patrol and the outside group. If one thing had become clear today, it was that we were potentially on thin ice with the police. For now, they were friendly and (mostly) accommodating toward us. It was critical that we stay out of their hair and not become a problem that they needed to solve.

> **BONNIE:** Hi gang—Ted and I would like to propose that beginning immediately he and I become the "point of contact" for any and all needs. Both what Pointe Patrol needs (i.e., food, ice, gas, etc.) and what those of us "outside" might need (i.e., Dottie meds). Then we will take the conversation off thread while we coordinate what needs to happen each day. Once daily we will ask Pointe Patrol how best to coordinate that day's rendezvous. Our hope is that this will free up some bandwidth for Wayne and the rest of Pointe Patrol. When Pointe Patrol posts a need here—Ted or I will take it and coordinate as above. Please if you aren't part of Pointe Patrol send requests / needs directly to Ted or myself.

She then posted both of their cell phone numbers so that everyone would have them.

> **TED:** Please remember, having Pointe Patrol in residence is a privilege that we need to respect. Thank you.

> **LAURA:** May I suggest we do a brief conference call this evening to set up systems, report on conditions, etc?

We all then went about our separate duties. I wandered around the neighborhood. On behalf of the owner, Bonnie asked about the house with the kicked-in door. It turned out that it was the fire department that had breached it so that they could save it should the fire from Per's house jump the fence. Better a smashed door than a destroyed house. A couple of the guys had gone in later and moved the sofa up against the front door to make it more difficult for looters to get in, and then they'd left out the back door.

Laura spent the rest of the afternoon organizing the conference call. She loves to organize things like that and is good at it. She had to do everything from her cell phone, but it didn't bother her. She was in her element.

Shortly after 4 p.m., Laura was ready and posted instructions to the thread.

> **LAURA:** Guys, we are going to have a Zoom meeting at 5 p.m. for anyone who wants to be there. You will get to hear reports from Dave on the fire, Wayne on looters, and Bonnie/Ted for the plan moving forward. You will have an opportunity to ask questions.

She then posted instructions on what software people needed to download in order to join the meeting and gave various technical details on how to connect, ending her post with:

> **LAURA:** See you there!!

As we approached 5 p.m., Laura went over to the café, where the rest of Pointe Patrol was. I had already logged into the meeting on my phone, and would have gone with her, but ended up getting sent over to Dave's house instead. He hadn't connected yet, and he might need tech support.

I knocked on his front door, and he opened it. Laura had been correct—Dave had been having trouble connecting to the meeting and was glad to see me. Rather than try to figure out what was going on with his phone, I just offered him mine, and he invited me in.

He went over to the breakfast table and put the phone down directly in front of him. He had a bunch of notes written out in red pen on note cards, which were stuck here and there on the table. Not wanting to disturb him, I simply stood in the kitchen by the counter and listened quietly.

Laura began the call, welcoming everyone. She made a few opening remarks and then told us that Wayne was there and ready to give an update about security.

Wayne spent the next few minutes discussing the issues with looters and how important it was not to lose focus and get lax. There had been looting throughout all the various evacuation areas, and despite an increased police presence, looters were still an issue and would continue to be so.

As Wayne gave us his report, Dave looked over and passed me a bag of cookies. They were new, and the bag was still sealed. Not wanting to interrupt Wayne, he made a silent gesture to indicate that I should open them and have one.

Opening that bag of cookies felt a lot like opening a candy wrapper in a movie theater. Sometimes it's not clear whether slow-and-quiet is better than fast-and-loud when it comes to opening noisy things in situations when you are supposed to be quiet, and this was one of those times. I chose slow-and-quiet and finally managed to get the bag open. I took a cookie and passed the bag over to Dave, who also had one. We munched in silence together as Wayne spoke.

"Thanks, Wayne," Laura's voice came on, after Wayne had completed his report. "Now we'll hear from Dave about the fires. Dave, are you there?"

Dave was on.

"Thanks, Laura. Before I begin... my wife has a collection of decorative stones on our deck, each painted with a word. They have been an inspiration to me the past few days, and I'd like to read them out to you all now."

He then paused and said each word slowly and with emphasis. "Believe. Joy. Love. Thanks. Faith. Gratitude.

"There were a number of things that happened in the past few days, any of which could have resulted in us losing the neighborhood. But each time, we were lucky, and somehow things always went in our favor. Someone out there is watching out for us, and I think that's because we have a very special neighborhood, made up of good people who care about each other. All of us have reason to think deeply about these words at this time."

Dave paused before continuing.

"Regarding the fire, three of the houses are a total loss, having been burned down to the foundations. These are the one on the corner and the two down at the end of the Q." He provided the addresses to be specific and so that there would be no confusion.

"Two houses have moderate damage and will need repairs and extensive clean up. These are Martha's and Ted's." Martha and Ted lived on either side of the one that burned down on the corner. The radiant heat from that fire had blown out both of their windows, deformed various parts of their walls, and in Martha's case, had even changed the color of her stucco.

"All the houses on the hill by Altruria have damage to their back-yards. Some of them have damage to their decks. But aside from that, none of them have any structural damage.

"All the other houses in the neighborhood aside from those that I have mentioned are in good condition."

He then gave an update on the situation regarding gas and electricity, shared what other mundane details about the neighborhood he thought might be interesting, and yielded the floor. No one had any questions, and the attendees in the outside group promised to pass along the information to people who had not been able to join.

After the meeting ended, Dave passed back my phone and thanked me for coming over. Bonnie was calling on Dave's cell, and I let myself out the front door to give them some privacy. As I made my way out, I heard her congratulate him, and I heard him start to complain about getting confused by the technology.

For dinner that night, Laura cooked spaghetti for everyone. We have a gigantic pot that you can almost fit an entire turkey into, which Laura unearthed from its regular place in the garage. She brought this over to the café and made use of the spaghetti noodles that had been part of our grocery delivery earlier.

Laura was cooking for eight hungry guys and herself, so she wanted to make sure there was enough for everyone to have as much as they wanted. She ended up going overboard, and we found ourselves with a mountain of spaghetti by the time she was through. We had sauce, bread, and lots of beer from the previous night, so we ate well.

The beer we had was good but not necessarily great. It was what Wayne was able to get his hands on in bulk at the grocery store. What I didn't know was that my companions were not regular beer drinkers. They were beer connoisseurs. Eddie and TJ even brewed it in their garage.

"Dude," Eddie said with a laugh, addressing Wayne. "What you need to get us is some Pliny."

Pliny—or more specifically, Pliny the Elder—is the name of a beer brewed by the Russian River Brewing Company. They have a brewery in downtown Santa Rosa, and every time I've driven by, there has been a long line to get in. It doesn't matter what time of day it is, there is always a line. Sometimes a small line, sometimes a large one, sometimes a line that wraps itself all the way around the building, but there's always a wait to get in. People come from all around the world to have a Pliny at the Russian River Brewery, and they're willing to stand in line to do it.

In beer circles, Pliny is considered by some to be the best beer in the world. Taste is a subjective thing, so there is obviously some disagreement. If you're from Belgium, chances are you believe a Belgian beer deserves that title. But if you're from California—Santa Rosa, in particular—then you have absolutely no doubt: Pliny is the best beer in the world. To be fair to the Belgians, or the stray American with defective taste buds, there may be disagreements about which specific beer is the very top spot, but there is universal agreement that Pliny is good enough to be in the discussion.

I had never tasted a Pliny before. It isn't something you can get at the grocery store. You can only get it at the Russian River Brewery, on tap at a few other local places, or through specialty distributors. To get one, you have to know what it is and specifically seek it out. Not being a huge beer drinker, and not willing to stand in line, I hadn't ever found myself in the position to drink one.

"Oh, you want a Pliny?" Wayne responded, with some sarcasm. He then stood up and started walking over to his house.

When Eddie understood what Wayne was up to, he got very worked up.

"Dude! No way!"

Wayne returned, holding two bottles of Pliny. They were the large, 16 oz. size. Wayne had gone and raided his own refrigerator to get them. Everyone at the table got excited.

Since there were nine of us, and only two bottles of beer, we had to share. Eddie got glasses for us all, and Wayne went around measuring out the Pliny, careful to make sure we all had our fair share.

We then made a toast—to Viewpointe Strong—and everyone clinked glasses. That's when I had my first Pliny. It was amazing. Even Laura liked it, and she doesn't like beer.

"This is what made me start to drink beer," Eddie said, sipping his beer off to the side. "I even started making my own after having Pliny."

"Liquid gold," TJ agreed.

Others voiced their appreciation as well. Dave seemed almost overwhelmed and didn't waste time with words. He sat there silently, enjoying the inch or so of Pliny that represented his share of Wayne's bounty. The next morning, he would report to us that he spent the whole night dreaming of it.

After finishing the Pliny, Laura and I didn't feel like drinking regular beer anymore, so we called it a night and headed home. We tended not to stay out quite as late as the others when it came to lingering after dinner. Having to feed the animals probably had something to do with that. Being the only married couple together at the circle probably contributed as well.

At about 9 p.m., Eddie texted to the Pointe Patrol thread.

### Pointe Patrol

**EDDIE:** Doing a quick patrol with TJ

A few minutes later, another text came through, this time from Sebastian.

**SEBASTIAN:** Any of you walking on Viewpointe by Dave and me?

**SEBASTIAN:** Just saw flashlights

**ME:** Eddie and TJ are patrolling

**SEBASTIAN:** Ok cool

**SEBASTIAN:** Wasn't sure, was about to come out

**LAURA:** Get em!!!!

**ME:** We will let Oscar run. He'll clear the streets

**TJ:** Just don't let Oscar out now, we're out here!!

**SEBASTIAN:** Just play dead

**ME:** If you have treats that helps

Eddie and TJ didn't come across anything in their patrol, and we all found ourselves gifted with the luxury of being able to sleep through the night a second time. Things felt like they were finally settling down.

# CHAPTER 12

# Party Time

SINCE WE DIDN'T have access to any newspapers or television up in the circle, the text thread became our primary lifeline to the outside world. It always seemed to get active first thing in the morning, when everyone shared any developments they had learned.

### #VIEWPOINTE STRONG

**TED:** Good morning Pointe Patrol

**WAYNE:** Sky Hawk and Rincon Valley under evacuation

**TED:** Mandatory?

**BONNIE:** Yes mandatory

**WAYNE:** A lot of Sonoma under mandatory evacuation

Although the fires in our immediate neighborhood had calmed down, that was not the case in surrounding areas. We may have been the first to evacuate, but we wouldn't be the last.

**ELLIOT:** Take a cold shower this morning looks like Governor and Senators will be touring damage today 😊

**TED:** Here? Or in DC?

**BONNIE:** 😄

**WAYNE:** 👆 Politicians

**NORMA:** Late news said they are touring here

**EDDIE:** Café is open. Coffee brewing

I used to wait for Eddie to send out the notification that the café had opened for the day. My coffee habit was officially back on.

**WAYNE:** I'll be there to arrest them it's a mandatory evacuation

**WAYNE:** Have your AR out you know Feinstein will love that. Lol

**EDDIE:** Oh Geez

**EDDIE:** What do Politicians and Looters have in common?

**WAYNE:** Everything

**EDDIE:** 😄

The gang seemed to be in good spirits this morning. We didn't usually start out with a round of jokes about politicians. The good vibes continued when a status message appeared in the text thread that Laura had added Dave to the conversation. I think it had become obvious to him, and to a lot of the other neighbors in the outside group, that being connected on the thread was a huge advantage. He was no longer going to be a cell phone hermit.

**BONNIE:** Wow Dave gave you permission to add him oh my gosh

**LAURA:** Lol. He did indeed! Actually asked to be in it 😄

**BONNIE:** Welcome sweetie I love you

**DAVE:** Love you

Of course, posting I-love-yous on a group text thread is a surefire way to invite some wisecracking at your expense.

**ELLIOT:** Keep it clean you two

**BONNIE:** Elliot you're so boring

**EDDIE:** Love you more

**TED:** Love you long time... oops!

**BONNIE:** 😂😂😂

By 10 a.m., Bonnie and Ted had gotten a list of most of the supplies needed for the day. Today the plan was to cover up all the broken windows in Ted's and Martha's houses with plastic, which required some supplies that weren't available in Gary's garage.

In addition to using the thread to organize supplies for Pointe Patrol, people in the outside group put in requests for us to go and get various things they had left behind and needed. Prescription medications were the primary concern. As people gave instructions to me, I'd go over to their houses and get the items they needed.

By 11:45, Bonnie was headed up, and I was headed down. We met at the Baldwin gate, which was our usual rendezvous point. Almost no one knew it was there, which meant that our group were usually the only ones present. That made it easier, especially when it came to interacting with the police. As usual, they were friendly.

Bonnie had a car loaded full of supplies and food. She backed it up to the gate, and I did the same on my side, and everything was transferred over. I made sure to give her the prescriptions I had retrieved from people's houses, and we gave each other a hug. Before she left, she made sure I understood that there was a special bag just for Dave. It contained his cigarettes and a six pack of beer for his private stash.

I made my way back up, and all the supplies were quickly unloaded and put in their place by the group. Bonnie and Ted had bought us bright yellow safety vests, similar to the one that Sebastian wore around. We figured that the extra visibility would help us stand out to each other as well as to the police compared to potential looters. Everyone put on a vest, and we felt pretty cool in our new uniforms. TJ wrote his name on the back of his in big letters with a permanent marker.

Laura's friend Amy had come up to help out for the day. I hadn't been sure if the police would let her through when Laura and I had gone down to pick her up, but as long as she was with us, they had been OK with it. We found her an extra vest—an orange one—and she got suited up as well. She had been going crazy listening to the news and wanted to help out in some way rather than just be a spectator. Once she had connected with Laura and found out what was going on at Viewpointe, this became the place she wanted to volunteer at. Today, that meant guarding the café and watching out for looters.

Laura, Amy, and Oscar went out to the middle of the street in front of the café and positioned themselves there as sentries. No one could get in or out without going through them. The rest of us headed over to Ted and Cathy's.

This was the first time I had been inside Ted's house since the fire. The bedroom was a mess. The bed itself was half-burned, and there was glass everywhere from where the heat from the burning house next door had blown in the windows. There was heavy soot and smoke damage throughout the house.

The weather report had called for rain in the next day or so, which everyone was extremely glad to hear. The problem was that with no windows, the two houses were vulnerable to being damaged even more than they already had been. Dave was adamant about getting plastic up over the open windows before that could happen.

We had a huge roll of clear plastic, and Ted's garage was transformed into a cutting room. When someone needed a piece of plastic cut, that person would take the measurements out to the garage. The team there would then cut the plastic to size. We had staple guns that we could use to attach the plastic to the wall, as well as a bunch of duct tape to seal the edges.

The first sign of trouble came after Gary and I cut a piece to put in Ted's bedroom window. Dave had been floating between everyone and didn't like our plastic.

"It has to be exactly to the edges, without going over," he said, pointing to the corners of the window. We had cut ours allowing an inch of overlap on all the sides. He didn't like it that way.

"You can do it however you want," Dave said when he saw our doubting looks. "But if you do it differently than this, I'm just going to come back later and do it again myself."

I've been in positions before where I had to deal with stubborn people. I used to be a project manager for a volunteer organization, and I remember having to fight tooth and nail to keep the group doing things efficiently and not getting side tracked. Just because Dave wanted it done just-so didn't mean that was the best way to go about it. I'm a woodworker, and Gary has a job in the hardware business. We're competent enough with our hands to hang up some plastic over a window. Arguments rose to my lips, but I thought twice and swallowed them down. Neither one of us wanted to argue with him.

Over the next few days, Dave ended up doing a lot more work himself than he would have otherwise because people would wander off their jobs to do something else rather than be micromanaged. No one held a grudge against him, though. It was his nature to be stubborn. We all knew that same stubbornness had also been responsible for preserving the neighborhood in the first place. "He's the Chief," we used to say to each other with a laugh.

Seeing the piece of plastic being re-cut and realizing there were plenty of people here to help without me, I made my way over to Martha's instead, where I found TJ, Eddie, and Fountainview Mike. Her windows had blown in as well, although nothing in her house had actually caught fire.

We made quick work of the large window in the dining room, and I wrote warnings on the plastic in marker. It was a long drop to the ground on the other side of the window, and the plastic gave a false sense of security since you couldn't see through it to know what was on the other side.

The most difficult one was the window halfway down the stairs. There were two flights of stairs, and the windows were located right above the landing between them. The top of this window was round, which meant we'd have to cut the plastic in a circle. What made all of it more difficult is that they were up high, and accessing them required climbing pretty high up a ladder.

Eddie wanted to get these windows done before Dave showed up. "I don't want to make him climb this ladder. He's done enough. He shouldn't have to do that," Eddie told me. I agreed.

After we had cut most of the plastic, Dave showed up to inspect our work.

"Good job," he told us, after looking over the dining room plastic. I breathed a sigh of relief. If he had told us to take it down because he didn't like it, I don't think I would have been able to bite my tongue a second time.

He then made his way over to help Fountainview Mike and Eddie with the windows on the stairs. There wasn't room down the stairs for me or TJ to fit, so we moved and went to work on covering the windows in the kitchen.

When TJ and I were through, I carried out some trash and checked on the other team at Ted's. They were done, and all that was left was the circular window at Martha's, which was well underway. We had beaten the rain, and water damage wouldn't be something Ted or Martha would have to add to their already long list of insurance claims.

What I didn't learn about until later that night was that there was some drama over those circular windows. What we all didn't realize was how good Dave was at moving up and down ladders, being an ex-firefighter. He knew to put all his weight right in the middle, and how to move smoothly from one rung to the other. Back in his day, he used to race other firefighters up and down ladders for fun. He declared that he could climb a ladder faster than any of us, and it didn't matter that he was the oldest person on Pointe Patrol and not in the best of shape anymore.

When Dave saw Eddie on the ladder, he didn't approve of Eddie's lack of technique. By putting his weight on the sides of the rungs, rather than in the middle, Eddie made the ladder sway too much. And his lack of confidence made him take things slower than Dave would have liked. Slow and dangerous: not a good combination in his mind.

It didn't take long before Dave told Eddie to get off the ladder. Eddie refused. Eddie had already made up his mind that he wasn't going to let Dave do any climbing.

This made Dave angry. Eddie was being slow and inefficient. He had refused to get off the ladder. But to make it worse, this was Dave's ladder. Dave had brought it over out of his own garage.

Dave moved quick, climbing up two steps on the ladder until he was just underneath Eddie. He had one of the construction staple guns in his hand, and he pressed it right up into Eddie's ass, between his two butt cheeks.

"Get the fuck off the ladder," Dave demanded through gritted teeth. Later on, Dave said he could feel Eddie clench through that staple gun.

Eddie, realizing this was a do-or-die moment, stayed true to his plan and climbed higher. I believe this time he moved with appropriate speed. The adrenaline probably helped.

Dave didn't follow, and the windows were finished without any issues. Eddie and Dave made up afterward and had a good laugh about the whole thing. There were quite a few stapler jokes told at dinner after that point.

By the time mid-afternoon rolled around, most of Pointe Patrol was relaxing at the café. A lot of us tended to come together around this time to visit while we charged our cell phones before nightfall. Laura and I had already dropped Amy off back at the Baldwin gate, thanking her for her help. As usual, we had chatted with the police officers down there, asking for any news they might have. We were always interested to see what they had come across that day, and if we learned anything, we'd post it to the thread.

## Pointe Patrol

**LAURA:** Looters on bicycle or foot. Milpitas PO on Baldwin

**WAYNE:** Several arrests made today on looters

**WAYNE:** Wikiup crawling with them

**WAYNE:** Lots of looting reports being dispatched to patrol

**ME:** Is it getting worse? Do we need to be doing night patrols for that?

**AMY:** Looter being arrested at corner of Mendo and Bicentennial when I was jumping on the 101.

Laura had added Amy to today's Pointe Patrol thread. She set up a new thread any time someone came or left on a particular day. Amy's report of the looter being arrested was right at the police line that Laura and I had walked up through on the very first day. I don't think it would be nearly as easy to get up here now as it was then.

As I sat at the table, Fountainview Mike was telling Sebastian about how he got his dogs.

"I went online and found a tool that tells you what breed fits your lifestyle the best. How big is your yard? How much exercise do you get? Do you have kids or not? Then it recommends the breed that best suits you. For us it was Westies. We've got two of them. One is a little crazier than the other, but they fit us perfectly." He was enthusiastic. People love talking about their dogs.

"Wait a minute," I said. "You have two Westies? Two little white dogs?"

"Yeah," Mike acknowledged. He had told me about the online breed tool before, but I hadn't connected the dots.

"Those were your two dogs that Oscar went after??"

"Yeah, that was them! I kind of thought it was you once you said you had a Doberman."

I was stunned by the coincidence. Mike's dogs were the two that had barked at Oscar, which resulted in Oscar chasing them down after his leash had broken. It was his daughter who had been walking them in front of my house and who had cussed me out and thrown up in my yard.

Initially, I had been a little mad at the owner of those two dogs. Now it turned out to be the guy I had been partnered up with on many of my patrols in the night. It was almost a cosmic joke how we had been thrown together like that. Talk about karma.

I relayed the story of what had happened between Oscar and Mike's two Westies to the rest of Pointe Patrol who had curiously been listening to our conversation, and we all had a good laugh about it. Thinking back to the previous day, I was especially touched with how Mike had let Oscar put his head in his lap, petting him and telling him how good of a boy he was. If there had ever been any bad feelings between Mike and me, they were long gone. He and I were brothers.

It was getting toward dinner time, and Wayne had just gotten off work. He sent a text as he got ready to head home.

### Pointe Patrol

**WAYNE:** Pliny?

**EDDIE:** Bro!!!!! Pliny!!!!!

And with that, we all waited expectantly for Wayne to return, like little kids waiting for Santa to come down the chimney on Christmas Eve.

We saw Wayne pull around the corner and into the circle. Rather than turning into his own driveway, he kept going straight and headed for the café. As he got closer, he sped up and turned on his sirens and lights. He came into the driveway and skidded to a halt, as if he were about to make some kind of bust. Even though we knew it was him, we still got a little bit of a start being approached aggressively like that.

When he got out, he was smiling. He was in a good mood. He made his way around to the back and started unloading Pliny. Whoever was near got handed a case. There were four cases of it and a big box of glasses.

He told us how he had managed to come into all this Pliny. Wayne is good at telling stories.

"I went over to the Russian River, and I think I stood out a little. All covered in dirt. They knew something was up. They were probably like, 'What happened to this guy?'

"When he came over, I said, 'I need to get some Pliny. I think I need to buy as much as you'll sell to me.'

"That seemed to confuse him a little, so I explained what we were doing. 'I've got this team, and we've been up in the burn zone for a week. Yesterday was the first day that we felt like we might really make it, and we had a little celebration with two bottles of Pliny. Each one of us had like this much…'"

Wayne held his hand up, with his finger about an inch away from his thumb, mimicking what he had said to the bartender at the Russian River.

"So we got to talking a little. And then afterward, he motions to another guy, and the two of them huddle together and start whispering and having a discussion. Then they come over with these four cases of Pliny and tell me that all of it is on the house.

"'What do you mean?'

"'It's free. Take it.'

"'I can't let you do that. How much do you want for it?'

"'Nothing. It is for you and your team.'

"'I can't just take it for free. I've got to pay you something.'

"'You can take it, or you can leave it, but you're not paying for this beer.'

"So we argued a little, and then I compromised by agreeing to buy all these beer goblets. Then they helped me load it up in the car, and we were like…"

Wayne acted out hugging people in the air, pretending to cry as he did it. I wondered if he really had cried in the moment. If anything would make him cry outside the neighborhood burning down, it would be something like someone giving him four cases of Pliny for free in recognition of what we'd all been through. Not only does the gang at the Russian River Brewing Company know how to brew some amazing beer, they also have huge hearts. What a beautiful gesture that was. And yet again, I found myself impressed with how Sonoma County residents and businesses pulled together during the fire.

So there we were: all alone in an evacuation zone, the entire neighborhood deserted except for us. No power, no gas; we were dirty and borderline exhausted. But we had each other, and we still had our homes. The neighborhood was safe—this was the first time that we really began to feel confident about that. We had a working makeshift café, and we had just scored a treasure trove of Pliny, the best beer in the world. There was only one thing left to do under those conditions! This was the beginning of what would become the most epic party I've ever been to.

It started off slow as Wayne passed out the beer goblets. We had invited the Gardenview group from a few streets up to join us, and a couple of them had wandered down. Glasses were clinked, and toasts were made. The Pliny began to flow freely.

One important thing to realize about Pliny is that it has twice the alcohol content of a regular beer. A little Pliny goes a long way. I realized I might be in trouble when TJ took it upon himself to go around and constantly top everyone's glass off. There was no way to tell how many glasses I had drunk, and at a certain point I stopped trying to count. Right about then, Eddie fired up the music.

Eddie had power to his desk from the generator, and he had some speakers set up there. He also had some DJ equipment that allowed him to cue songs up and mix them in the same way you'd experience at a club.

I don't know what the police officers thought as they'd drive by on their patrols. We had the flood lights illuminating the whole street, music blaring, and people laughing and making too much noise. We'd always wave and offer them a beer, but they were on duty and could never take us up on our offer. They'd only laugh and wave back, then continue on their routes. I heard later that one of them said something to the effect of, "There's not even supposed to be anyone up here, but these guys are having a block party."

Ted checked in. He had heard about the Pliny.

## #VIEWPOINTE STRONG

**TED:** How's the Pliny?

**DAVE:** OUTSTANDING. Testosterone dinner party going on here with 12 people. Sitting outside under the stars doing our best to laugh and de-stress for a few hours and then return to our routine.

**TED:** 12? WTF? Did y'all bring dates?

**BONNIE:** Yeah really your group is growing?

**ME:** Visitors from the Gardenview group

**BONNIE:** 👍

**NICOLE:** Dates.... Whatever it takes to keep the group going!

**LAURA:** They are pretty ugly ;)

**ME:** We're all pretty drunk tho 😄

**BONNIE:** hmmmmmm... and I'm stuck down here?? 😒

**SEBASTIAN:** Drink more, beer goggles are a real thing.

**NICOLE:** So is the morning after 😳

Laura had been impressed that Dave had taken to group texting so well, given how anti-technology he had been in the beginning. She noticed that he seemed to be having multiple conversations going at once.

**LAURA:** FYI: y'all Dave and Bonnie are sexting. Gross.

**BONNIE:** 😂 😂

**BONNIE:** Sadly I'm awfully sober 🙄

**DENISE:** Laughter is a great healer—enjoy and stay safe!! ❤️
🙏

**BONNIE:** It is 🖤

**TED:** Stay safe tonight Pointe Patrol!!!

**DAVE:** We're cherishing the moment all. Back to work as usual after.

Laura and I were standing together out on the grass when Wayne came over to us. We all had our glasses in our hands.

"I've got to say, I was kind of surprised when you two first showed up. The yoga people?"

We laughed. Laura and I both practiced yoga, but I didn't realize that this was a known fact about us. I thought it was funny that Wayne thought of us as the "yoga people."

"And then you show up with the kick ass dog…. The yoga people have that dog? And a gun… ? The yoga people have a gun!?" Every time he said "yoga people," his voice went higher in mock surprise. We were all laughing.

"I guess you need to rethink your stereotypes," I told him. Obviously, in Wayne's eyes, we had been just another couple of California libtards, doing yoga, smoking pot all day, and generally making the country a worse place with our out-of-control progressiveness.

"I guess I do!" he agreed.

After talking with Wayne, I made my way into the garage to see what Eddie was up to. He was busy away at his DJ booth and turned to look at me. He was going to say something, but we just hugged instead.

"This is big," he said.

"I know. Not just big for the moment, but big for your life," I agreed. We all realized that our time at Pointe Patrol represented a peak experience. Those don't happen too often in a typical life. It's important to recognize them when they come. We paused for a few brief moments of silence thinking about that together, taking it all in, and then both laughed and returned to the music.

Laura had requested a song from Pink Martini, the same one that we had choreographed our wedding dance to ten years earlier. She and I made our way out to the street and began to rumba. Ten years ago, we had been awesome at this and had learned a bunch of moves in the dance classes we had taken at the time. Now, without practice, and both a little too drunk, we did our best to fake it but mostly just stumbled around. It didn't matter.

At a certain point, we ended up lying in a pile in the street. I'm not sure exactly how it happened, but it definitely did. I was on the bottom, and she was on top of me. The euphoria of the moment had overcome us.

> **DAVE:** We are having a moment here! Earik and Laura are down on the ground in the middle of the street laughing and hugging 😁
>
> **TED:** Is that TMI?
>
> **DAVE:** Hmmmmm
>
> **JOE:** Let those young'ns go 🙈
>
> **WAYNE:** Pointe Patrol is off the Mo-Fuk-en hook tonight... good luck looters!!!!
>
> **NICOLE:** I'm calling dispatch

After the song had finished, Laura and I got up and rejoined the group at the tables. Eddie started playing some Beastie Boys songs, and Wayne began to dance.

"I grew up on this shit!" he said. Not only was he dancing, he was singing along. I was surprised that he seemed to know every word to every song.

> **DAVE:** We're in trouble now! Wayne is dancing up a storm.
>
> **TED:** Videos please!!
>
> **KELLY:** Yes videos please we need entertainment

I started filming Wayne through my phone. When he saw me, he came over and played to the camera, singing right at me. He'd act out the lyrics as he sang them, not missing a beat. I was impressed. Dave also recorded from the side.

I posted the video to the group, as did Dave.

**ME:** Wayne the rapper 😊

**TED:** OMG! Is that Puffy or Wayne?

**DAVE:** God help us. That's Wayne

**ME:** That's the guy with the gun 😵

**DAVE:** Sorry all. This is way better than any Happy Hour party!!!

Dave was referring to our monthly neighborhood get-togethers, which were overwhelmingly pedestrian compared to what we had going on at Pointe Patrol.

**KELLY:** You guys are awesome!!!!!

**HOLLY:** Viewpointe's got talent

Wayne then sent a video of Eddie doing his DJ thing in the back of the garage. He had headphones on his head, but only covering one ear. As he spun tunes for us out of his mixer, he was dancing with one arm in the air, twirling the other next to him. He was still wearing his reflective orange safety vest.

**NICOLE:** Are we supposed to vote?

**DAVE:** Best decompression party ever. We all need this.

**NORMA:** Party 🎉 on Pointe Patrol! You've earned it.

Eventually, the party began to wind down and people started going home. Fountainview Mike had been the first to go. He had actually left before things got really crazy. Laura was next, followed by one of the Gardenview guys. That guy looked awfully wobbly to me, but he seemed to think he'd be able to make his way home back up the hill in the dark without ending up passed out in a ditch somewhere. We had all gone a little farther than we had intended with the Pliny.

It was getting late, and I was ready to turn in, too. I started to say my goodbyes but stopped. It was the unmistakable smell of fresh smoke. A few of us made our way out to the entrance to the circle, and the smell got stronger. Something was definitely burning.

Dave closed off the conversation with the larger group as the rest of us went and got our flashlights.

**DAVE:** Good night from Viewpointe Circle. Strong smell of smoke now. All going around area to investigate.

Like a pack of beagles chasing the scent of a fox, we headed out, following the scent. We walked down Altruria, then doubled back and made our way to the Boulders. We followed the walkway that led up from the lower parking lot to the upper one and found ourselves right back at the same spot where we had been a couple nights ago. This time, instead of the mulch by the tree smoldering, it was a big section down toward the ditch.

"The Boulders? Again!?" someone said.

No one was in the mood for another round of putting out mulch fires through the night. Fire trucks had been stationed in the area the past few days, and Wayne called 911 to get one here. We were glad when dispatch told us that one was on the way.

If we had learned anything in the past few days, it was that the destiny of the neighborhood was in our hands, and if we needed a job done, we were ultimately the ones that would have to do it. We fully expected a truck to come, but we weren't going to sit around while we waited for it. But having gone through this once before, we thought maybe there would be an easier way to deal with the fire than getting out the buckets.

The Boulders is a very large apartment complex, with multiple freestanding buildings. They are all connected with paths, and it's easy to move from one building to the next. There were fire extinguishers mounted at regular intervals throughout all the buildings, located on the walls behind glass. If there was ever a time to break the glass and use the extinguishers, this was it.

Sebastian went to one building, and Gary went to another. I stayed and walked the perimeter of the smoldering area to try to identify the edges. This was a large patch of mulch that was burning. I had been within feet of this spot countless times and had never noticed it. It had been quietly smoldering for almost a week now and had chosen this moment to finally burst into open flame.

Eventually, I went to see what everyone was doing, as it seemed like things were taking a long time. I found Gary at the first floor of one of the buildings. He was in front of the fire extinguisher and was trying to break the glass with the piece of metal dangling from a chain, which had been put there for that purpose. The glass wasn't breaking, and Gary was hitting it really hard. If he struck with any more force than he was already using, he would most likely get seriously injured.

I had always been a fan of my big blue flashlight for the beam of light that it cast in the dark. Now I was able to put it to another use. It is made of metal and has a very heavy, sturdy feel to it. In an emergency, when blunt force is needed, it was the perfect tool.

I smashed the glass with the back end of the flashlight, and it shattered. Shards flew everywhere, and one of them cut the side of my hand. This is the problem with breaking glass when drunk. I ignored the cut, and Gary pulled the extinguisher out.

TJ was one flight of stairs up, trying to break the glass on another extinguisher. Like Gary, he wasn't having any luck. When I came upon him, he had a huge rock in his hands that he had gotten from below and was standing ten feet away from the glass. He was preparing to heave that rock into the glass so he could get to the extinguisher.

Rather than letting TJ pitch his boulder, I went over and broke the glass myself. I regretted doing that, since he had gone through all the trouble of getting the rock and figuring out a strategy for breaking the glass. I'd apologize to him later, but at that point I was drunk, bleeding, and just trying to get things done.

We got the two extinguishers back down to the burning mulch, and Sebastian showed up with a couple more. I gave mine to the other guys, who were eager to spray down the mulch. Rather than bleeding all over my clothes, I sucked on my hand waiting for the blood to clot.

The first extinguisher failed to work. It was empty! So was the second.

"Are you kidding me?" someone said.

Not only had the glass been impossible to break, but the extinguishers behind the glass had been empty. I was stunned. Either the manufacturer had provided shoddy equipment or some maintenance person hadn't been doing their job. Either way, in a different situation, this could have cost people their lives. Why bother mounting fire extinguishers if they aren't actually filled with any repellant?

Thankfully, the third one was operational, and we were able to spray down the mulch. Fire extinguishers might work on an open flame, but they do a poor job of putting out a mulch fire. We just seemed to coat the mulch white, but it still kept smoldering. This wasn't going to work. We needed water.

In the interests of preparedness, we had already connected two long garden hoses into one giant one, and it was sitting right in Gary's front yard in case we needed it. Everyone else went to get that hose and some shovels, and I stayed back to monitor the situation and wait for the fire truck.

To keep everyone in the loop who might not know what was going on, I gave an update to the Pointe Patrol thread.

### Pointe Patrol

**ME:** We've got embers at the boulders

**ME:** I'm up here keeping an eye on it

It seemed like it took the others a really long time to get back to me. I think we'd have been a lot more efficient had this happened before the party rather than after it.

I was happy to see Eddie, Sebastian, TJ, and Gary appear. I expected them to drive, but they were walking up, carrying the gear they needed with them. Unlike my lightweight, expandable hose from the previous night, the one they had was heavy and awkward. It was too much for one person to carry alone; it took two or three people to do it with any ease.

When we had first smelled the smoke, Eddie had been in his garage playing music. He was so involved that he hadn't realized that the rest of us left. At a certain point, he looked up to find that everyone was gone, and he was all alone. But rather than find out what was going on, he chose to keep the party going and continued playing music anyway. One of the gang had dragged him away from his DJ setup when they went down to get the supplies. We all had a good laugh about that the next morning.

Having gone through the process once already, it was pretty easy a second time. We already knew where all the water spigots were, and Eddie had become an expert on turning them on and off. We ran a hose from the closest spigot down to the burning mulch area, and someone soaked it while another person raked the mulch to make sure the water got underneath.

Putting the fire out took some time, and I was concerned that there might be other areas that also had flared up over the last couple days. I thought it would be a good idea to double-check, so I retraced my steps from the night before. I walked the perimeter of the mulch areas, which took me between the first two buildings, and then around the back side of the others.

I passed all the areas we had doused a couple nights ago and was glad to see that there were no signs of any other smoldering spots. It took me some time, but I worked my way down to the second parking lot without discovering any new fires. That was good news. We would not be out here until the wee hours of the morning again. I sent an update to Pointe Patrol before heading back.

**ME:** I'm at the far end. Coming back

As I got closer to where the others were, I heard Eddie calling my name. He was relieved when I walked up.

"Dude, you can't just take off by yourself like that! I was worried about you."

"Oh. Sorry…" I thought I had told them where I was going before I left, but it looked like no one had heard. Blame the Pliny for that one. Or blame my own impulsiveness. Dave isn't the only one who can be stubborn. Eddie was probably right about being alone at night, and I admit that I did have a few creepy feelings at the back side of the apartments.

We gathered up the supplies and arranged the hose in big loops so that three people could get under it to make it easy to carry. We headed back to the circle, walking down the middle of Altruria. The fire truck never showed up.

As we got closer to Fountainview, we spotted a single flashlight in the streets. When we shined one of ours in its direction, the flashlight went out. Someone was on Fountainview, and they didn't want to be seen. We dropped our equipment and quickly jogged toward where we had seen the light. I texted Pointe Patrol as I went.

**ME:** Unidentified person

It would not have been good for a looter to meet up with our group just then. A bunch of drunk guys, all amped up, carrying shovels and heavy flashlights. That would have been like running into an angry mob. Things could escalate fast in a situation like that, and not in a good way.

Despite looking hard, we couldn't find anyone. Someone texted Fountainview Mike, who checked out his window and didn't see anything either. I called Wayne.

Wayne answered, and I told him what we had seen. He laughed and said that it was him, and that we could stand down. He had done a quick patrol up Fountainview while he had been waiting for us.

**SEBASTIAN:** Person identified, we're clear

As we returned to where we dropped the hose, the conversation turned to whether or not Wayne had really been doing a patrol, or whether he had just been messing with us. Most of us were strongly leaning toward the latter possibility.

That was everyone's last patrol of the night. Once I got home, I crashed. I suspect the others did as well. The text thread would start up a bit later than usual the next morning.

# CHAPTER 13

# TJ Gets Rolled

BONNIE WAS THE first to send something over the thread the next morning.

**#VIEWPOINTE STRONG**

**BONNIE:** Good morning gang how are the hangovers?

**BONNIE:** Dave's last post had us a tad concerned because he said there was a lot of smoke smell in the area

**EDDIE:** What hangovers?

**ME:** Mulch at the apts was burning again. We dealt with it

**BONNIE:** Good Lord I thought they had somebody up there to get that taken care of. You guys are amazing

Eddie hadn't been accurate about the hangovers—they were for real, and everyone had one. We all were dragging that morning. At least, everyone at breakfast was dragging. Gary almost moaned when I greeted him. Wayne had left early, as usual, before any of the rest of us had gotten up. His next text to Pointe Patrol indicated that he might have fared better than the rest of us.

## **Pointe Patrol**

**WAYNE:** You fuckers better save me a Pliny tonight

We hadn't gone through all the Pliny. There were still a few bottles left over.

After breakfast, Laura and I headed back to our house, planning to take Oscar on one of his patrols around the neighborhood. Before we got there, a white pickup truck pulled into the circle. By this point, all of us were hyper-sensitive of anyone that we didn't recognize. As the truck drove past the café, I could see everyone stop talking and go on high alert.

The truck drove past us and then made its way over to Ted's house at the far end of the circle and stopped. Laura and I were closest, and we got to him before any of the others. As Laura asked the driver questions, I took pictures of his license plate.

The man introduced himself as Shawn. He was in town from Nebraska, doing contracting work and restoring downed power lines, which gave him access to the evacuation zone. He said that he met Ted and Cathy at the hotel bar the previous night, and Ted had told him our story and showed him some of the videos from our party. He was familiar with Wayne's now infamous rap video that had been making the rounds.

By now, other members of Pointe Patrol had shown up and continued grilling Shawn. It had become clear that Shawn wasn't a looter, and he happily answered all of our questions. He told me that I could delete the picture of his license plate, as we didn't need to worry about him. Most people don't like it when you take their picture without permission. That's one of the reasons why we were so blatant about doing it.

Shawn had never been to Viewpointe Circle before, so he initially headed to Ted's house to get his bearings. Now that he saw that it was a small circle, he drove around and came to a stop in front of the café. He brought us gifts. He unloaded beer, ice, and some whiskey. It wasn't the cheap stuff either. One of the bottles was a large jug of Johnny Walker Blue Label, which costs $400 a bottle. Shawn had paid for all of it out of his own pocket.

Sebastian took a picture and posted it to the thread.

**SEBASTIAN:** Shawn met Ted and Cathy at the hotel bar. He delivered us ice, whiskey, and beer. Wished us all good luck. Great guy.

**BONNIE:** 👍

**TED:** Awesome guy! Glad he found you guys!!

Shawn would swing by the café frequently over the next few days, bringing us ice and checking in on how we were doing. The generosity we had experienced from the community wasn't limited to just Sonoma County residents. It appeared that it extended all the way to Nebraska.

After Shawn had left and we put away all of his gifts, TJ informed us that he was going to head out for a hot shower. The national guard had started showing up and had replaced the police at various checkpoints. TJ's parents had asked the guardsmen if TJ could come down for a shower and then return, and they replied that they had no problem with him doing that.

I understood what TJ was feeling. Out of all the things that we had been doing without, hot showers were by far the most missed. TJ's parents were waiting at the bottom of the hill for him now, ready to give him a ride back to their place.

"Just remember to get back up here before curfew," someone told TJ. He had plenty of time, though. It wasn't even noon. We waved goodbye to him, and he walked out of the circle, taking a right and heading down Altruria. He was in good spirits, walking with a spring in his step.

A text came through the Pointe Patrol thread. It had only been a minute since TJ had gone.

### Pointe Patrol

**SEBASTIAN:** Police are questioning TJ

**SEBASTIAN:** I can see it from my place

**LAURA:** He has ID

The police were out in force today. Fountainview Mike already had to show his ID to them twice. We all made sure we had our IDs at all times, just in case.

**SEBASTIAN:** It's SRPD

**SEBASTIAN:** My ID has another address so I don't want to go down there

Another minute or so passed. Then:

**SEBASTIAN:** They have him in hand cuffs

**SEBASTIAN:** Down on Altruria

**SEBASTIAN:** Behind my house

Getting questioned by police was to be expected. We all had to run that gauntlet from time to time just being up here. What I didn't expect was for anyone to get cuffed or arrested.

**ME:** Holy shit

**SEBASTIAN:** I just heard, you're not going back

Laura and I were at home, but I thought maybe I could vouch for TJ, so I headed over to Sebastian's place. I thought about going into his backyard and calling down to them, but he met me at the door and let me inside. His expression told me that he was concerned. We went into his kitchen, where he had the blinds half-closed.

"Don't move the blinds," Sebastian warned. It was clear that he didn't want the police to know we were there. We could see three officers. TJ was sitting on the sidewalk, looking down. The body language and feel of the interaction wasn't friendly.

**WAYNE:** Wouldn't you? he looks like a thug 😂

**WAYNE:** Calm down it will be fine

**EDDIE:** True dat

I began to rethink my original idea of yelling down at the police from Sebastian's yard. That might not be the best idea given the mindset of these particular cops. Sebastian certainly seemed to be spooked.

We watched for a while, and then I had seen enough. I wasn't going to be able to do anything from here. I headed home.

**SEBASTIAN:** I'm just thinking we're all about to get booted

**LAURA:** Says the white guy

Laura had a point. Fountainview Mike and I had been stopped by police more than once and never had any issues. I had even been open carrying a firearm during one of those encounters. TJ hadn't even made it half a block out of Viewpointe and he was already in cuffs.

**WAYNE:** Is it code 4 yet?

None of us knew what that meant.

**SEBASTIAN:** They took him, probably escorting him out

**FOUNTAINVIEW MIKE:** Seriously??

That was quick. The neighborhood was no longer the deserted wasteland that we had all become used to over the last week. Now it felt like we were on lockdown in a war zone.

**WAYNE:** Why is the Mexican with a flat brim hat out walking the hood?

**SEBASTIAN:** Yep

**ME:** He was trying to leave. He was going to meet his parents and take a shower

**LAURA:** His parents were picking him up for a hot shower. They cleared it with the national guard. He was going to come back after

**SEBASTIAN:** Stay put, they are now with Dave and Ed

I had seen Dave and Eddie walking toward the entrance to the circle. I wasn't sure if they had decided to go down to the police or wait for them to come up. Laura and I were at home, following the drama by text. It didn't seem safe to go outside.

**TJ:** Yeah it's stupid. They said if I come back, they'll take me to jail

They must have taken TJ down to his parents and let him go. I was glad that he hadn't been arrested. He wouldn't have been able to text us otherwise.

> **ME:** Keep me posted. I was going to guard the café, but maybe I'll just hang out for a bit
>
> **WAYNE:** Have cop call me
>
> **TJ:** Well I told him I knew Wayne and he said he'll give you a call

The hardest part about getting live updates to an important event via text is sitting and waiting for new information. I'm pretty sure everyone in the group had their phones in hand at this moment. Wayne sent the next message. It wasn't good.

> **WAYNE:** Go inside and hide now
>
> **WAYNE:** TJ was on probation and then lied about it so police flooding area right now. Pull down garage door go inside

That was not a text anyone wanted to see. Laura and I took Oscar up to our bedroom and closed the door. We didn't want Oscar to start barking if a police car drove by the house. Sebastian and Gary might be able to lie low and hide in their houses, but Oscar freaking out would be a dead giveaway in our case.

> **SEBASTIAN:** They're in Viewpointe
>
> **SEBASTIAN:** In front of Norma's
>
> **SEBASTIAN:** I'm staying low

The police had moved up into the circle. How many of them were there? Were they going to go door to door and find all of us? Our bedroom doesn't have a window to the front of the street, so with the door closed we had no idea what was going on aside from what Sebastian reported. I had a vision of a squadron of police and the national guard working their way through the neighborhood, pulling us out of our houses like so many weeds in a garden.

> **ME:** What if they knock?

**ME:** If they do, Oscar will bark and I'm SOL.

SOL stands for *shit out of luck*. I realized how precarious my situation was. All it would take is one knock on the door, and Oscar would give our position away. He doesn't understand the concept of hiding. I didn't like it either. My instincts told me that my best option would be to go outside and talk to the police and try to explain the situation. Hiding seemed like exactly the wrong approach. Had Wayne not specifically told us to hide, I'd have already been out there.

**SEBASTIAN:** SRPD just showed up

**SEBASTIAN:** They're showing them something on Ed's cell

I didn't know if that meant the police had seized Eddie's cell, or if Eddie was there with them. If they had Eddie's phone and were looking through the pictures, they'd know exactly how many of us there were up here. We had all taken a ton of pictures of each other. The cars in most of our driveways didn't help either—they were flags that would tell anyone with half a brain which houses were occupied.

**WAYNE:** I think he's going to sort it out I know him he's cool we just talked

**ME:** Should I go down and talk?

**ME:** Might be better

I was having trouble sitting still. I felt like I needed to be outside to help things from going sideways just in case.

**TJ:** I totally forgot about my DUI charge man... I fucked up guys

**SEBASTIAN:** They're calling someone

**ME:** If we hide they'll just come back later. I really think I should go out there. Wayne?

I gave Wayne about ten seconds to respond but didn't hear anything back. I couldn't wait any longer. I was going out.

**ME:** Ok. I'm going

"If Sebastian says that I get arrested, just load the animals up and put them in the car and be ready to leave," I told Laura. The absolute last thing that we wanted was for Oscar to go after some police officer who was trying to remove Laura from the house. If I got taken out of the neighborhood, she'd still have time to get Oscar and the cats in the car and be ready to go voluntarily. The police would understand that situation.

I headed out. I removed my pocket knife and left it behind, just in case the cops were extra suspicious. I wasn't sure how many there would be, or what their mindset was. They didn't sound friendly.

As I walked out the door, I looked down both ends of the street. It was empty. That was good. It would make Laura's job easier if she had to get Oscar loaded.

I made my way over to Norma's, which was on the other side of the circle. I saw Eddie there, talking with three police officers. He was showing them something on his phone. As I approached, I greeted them and was relieved to see that they all appeared calm.

There was one older officer who seemed to be the one in charge. The other two wore helmets and armor and were huge. I consider myself to be a tall person, and in an average crowd I'm usually one of the taller people present. Those two cops made me look short. They were giants. With all their armor and equipment, it felt like I was standing in front of two huge football linebackers. If those two wanted to put someone in handcuffs, that person was going to get put in handcuffs. There would be no way to fight them off.

It was clear almost immediately that they understood the situation, and that they weren't going to give us trouble. I was friendly to them, and they were friendly back. My nervous tension immediately began to subside.

The older officer told me, "The helicopter saw you all and thought you were looting someone's garage. There were ten cops headed up here when we caught your friend."

After Shawn left, a helicopter had flown over the circle. It had passed over us quite low, so we definitely noticed it but didn't think anything of it at the time. From their perspective, they would have seen four or five guys with reflective work vests moving things in and out of an open garage. They had thought we had broken into Eddie's house and were clearing it out. No wonder TJ had been seized right away. He had fit the exact description of the looters and had even been wearing a backpack with a laptop computer inside. Now it all started to make more sense.

"So you thought we were looters," I said to one of the giants. "Have you caught any others up here?"

"Yeah, we find all kinds of people. Some of them wear disguises and pretend that they have a reason to be here."

The vests didn't seem to be having the effect on cops that we had thought. They were viewing them as a disguise.

"Do you think we shouldn't be wearing these vests? Do we look like looters with them?" I asked.

"Well, no, you don't look a scumbag looter." Then he paused. It felt like he was weighing his words. "But if we see you, we have to stop you." Maybe being seen wasn't such a good idea. There's no easier way to be spotted than to wear a bright yellow reflective vest around all day, and all of us were doing that. I wonder how much those vests had contributed to the helicopter coming in for a closer look. Today would be the last day any of us wore them.

The five of us chatted for a few minutes longer, and then I shook their hands and left. We were going to be fine. As I walked home, I checked my phone. I had felt a number of texts come through, but I didn't want to be rude and check when I was talking with the cops.

**WAYNE:** Yes

**WAYNE:** I've been out of cell coverage

**WAYNE:** Thank them for jamming up TJ it's what they should be doing after all remember

**TJ:** I was just outside the area and national guard said I could come down as long as I have my ID that's what they told my parents.

**TJ:** I tested the waters and it was a terrible idea. I'm so sorry

**SEBASTIAN:** I think we will be ok

**LAURA:** Me too. I am going to leave soon. I need a couple days before I go to work and deal with traumatized patients! Those that are staying, please get Viewpointe in shape for families to move home and have hope!! It has been an honor to be in your company this past week! Thank you all so very deeply.

Laura had been thinking about leaving all morning. Now that the fires were under control and the neighborhood was safe, she felt she could make a bigger difference at her job. Like TJ, I also think she heard the siren song of a hot shower calling to her.

**ME:** We're fine. You can come out if you want

**ME:** Those cops were huge!

**LAURA:** But little puppies on the inside

**ME:** TJ—don't beat yourself up. That helicopter reported us. They thought we had your garage open and were cleaning out the house.

**ME:** 10 cops were on their way up to deal with it when you got caught

**GARY:** I am staying inside

Gary wasn't going to take any chances with those cops. He was going to lie low in his house until all the police left the neighborhood. There was no car in his driveway, and no dog to bark at someone at the door. It would be hard for anyone to know he was there if he didn't want to be discovered.

**ME:** Lol. They were cool after we talked

**GARY:** Sounds good

**SEBASTIAN:** We have an important question for you TJ, who gets to drink your Pliny? ;)

That text was the signal that everyone had calmed down.

**TJ:** I'm on my way to pick it up right now! ;P

**SEBASTIAN:** Too late, Ed is already back to the DJ booth!

**TJ:** Haha we'll see.

**GARY:** Only 2 bottles are left

**WAYNE:** I get 1

After the police had left, I got Oscar ready for a patrol and we headed out. The neighborhood was extra quiet, and it was the first time I had seen Eddie's garage door pulled down during the day.

As I passed by, Eddie called to me from his doorway. Oscar and I stopped, and we went over. Gary had seen us from across the street and came over as well.

"Do you guys want to come in?" Eddie asked.

"Sure," Gary said.

"Can I bring Oscar?" I wasn't just going to walk in with Oscar without permission.

"As long as he doesn't take a shit on the carpet," Eddie replied.

I vouched for Oscar's bathroom manners, and we went inside. Eddie and Gary sat on the couch by the stairs, and I took a chair across from them. I told Oscar "*down*" and he sprawled out on the floor to my side. Sebastian showed up right after we all sat down and made his way to another chair by the front window. All the shades were down.

The fact that Oscar rested his head completely flat on the ground and went to sleep showed how comfortable he had become with the group. He trusted everyone here, and they trusted him. I didn't take his leash off and let him run freely, but at the same time I wasn't worried about him causing any trouble either.

"I can't believe TJ got rolled," Eddie said. He was visibly upset about what had happened.

"I know…. Do you think he got profiled?" I asked. My encounters with the police outside the circle had all felt totally different than this one.

"He totally got profiled," Eddie said. "I should have been there for him. I shouldn't have let him go."

"Well, you can't lie to cops, though. He wasn't honest about his probation when they asked," Sebastian said. "Joe's son tried to get up here by lying to the police and telling them that his father was stranded in the house. When they drove him up and found that no one was there, they got really mad at him and just took him back out again." I had heard about this but hadn't actually seen it happen.

"Once you tell them one lie, they don't trust anything else you say," Gary agreed.

"He didn't lie to them. He probably got stressed out and didn't know what they were asking. I live here with my girls, and there's no way I would bring anyone into this house that I couldn't completely trust. I trust TJ. One hundred percent. He's a good person. It was my responsibility to look out for him and I let him down," Eddie said.

We were all silent for a moment. Whatever justification the police had for cuffing TJ and driving him out of the area, we all felt that it was an injustice. TJ had spent the last week putting out fires and trying to save the neighborhood. He didn't deserve to be treated like a common looter.

"I'm not going to wear that vest anymore," I said, breaking the silence. I noticed that the others had taken theirs off as well.

"Me either," Gary replied. "I think from now on we probably need to stay in the circle and not venture out."

We all agreed. The police had really stepped up their presence in the area, and if we kept on roaming around outside the circle, it was only a matter of time before another one of us got forcibly removed from the neighborhood. From now on, we were going to lie low and try to keep out of the way of law enforcement. The environment was different now, and we no longer had the same level of autonomy that we did in the early days.

After we left Eddie's, Sebastian posted a number of pictures he had found online. Police officers were standing over a pile of loot arranged on the sidewalk. Ten iPhones were lined up next to a bunch of other valu-ables, such as watches and jewelry. A very intimidating looking handgun with a scope was shown in an open case. In the background, there was a bike on its side. This must have come from one of the looters on bikes that had been making their way through the neighborhoods. It may have even been one of the guys on the mountain bikes that Oscar growled at.

## #VIEWPOINTE STRONG

**SEBASTIAN:** SRPD busted a looter in NW Santa Rosa. Look how much stuff he had with him!

**BONNIE:** 😠

**BONNIE:** that gun looks scary

**WAYNE:** Competition target shooting, lots of money in that gun.

**WAYNE:** Lots of looting arrests and a lot more looters from out of the area where there is not enough probable cause to make arrest.

**WAYNE:** We have the best system money can buy. It's not what you know... it's what you can prove.... Plus we have jury panels full of LIBTARDS who use emotion not common sense

Wayne's frustration came through in his text. Out of all of us, he seemed to despise looters the most, and it must have been hard for him to see them being caught and released to the extent that they were.

As the afternoon wore on, Laura and I heard a vehicle pull into the circle. We made our way outside and saw a large red truck on the other side of the street. It was bigger than a regular pickup and looked almost like a miniature fire truck. We made our way over to it, and I noticed Montana license plates. The last time I saw a fire truck with Montana plates, I had been face-to-face with two would-be looters.

"Hi there," I said to the driver, who had his window down.

"Hi," he replied. "We're here on behalf of insurance. We need to check on this house." Déjà vu. This time, I would not be as easily fooled as I was before.

"OK. We've had a lot of looters come through here. Do you mind if we take pictures?" I asked. Laura had already taken a picture of the license plate and took a few more of the truck. Even though I asked permission, it didn't matter what he said. We were definitely going to be taking pictures of him.

"Sure! Take as many as you like. Take a picture of that. That's the number that identifies us," he pointed to the DOT number on the side of his vehicle. Laura came over and snapped a picture of it.

There were a lot of similarities between these two guys and the "Valley Fire" looters we had met a few days ago. They both said they worked for insurance, coming to check on a particular house. They both drove in fire trucks with Montana license plates. They all wore yellow jump suits. But once I started looking for differences, they were stark.

Rather than wearing brand-new yellow jumpsuits like the looters had, these guys looked like they had been living in theirs. They were dirty and well worn. Both men had grit under their fingernails, and both sported big, bushy beards. They had the tired look of two people who had been working very hard without a lot of sleep. In some ways, they reminded me of a gnarly version of my Pointe Patrol companions. They talked straight, were to the point, and had absolutely no problem being interrogated. They represented the real deal, whereas the looters had been the cheap knockoff.

The driver showed me his identification. His buddy got out of the truck and started filling out some paperwork against the side of it. It was pretty clear that the house they were interested in was not in any immediate danger.

"Have you guys put out any fires?" I asked.

The guy outside the truck answered first. "When we get sent out to houses, a lot of times there is smoldering in the backyard, or embers that the fire department missed. When we see that, we put it out ourselves. We've saved a few houses that way. That's why insurance sends us out."

The driver chimed in once his partner had finished. "Back before this gig, we were both firefighters. We've been fighting fires our whole lives."

We shared some of our story with them, and they nodded appreciatively. They understood what we had been through. They had been through similar situations themselves.

When they were content that the house they had come for was safe, the second guy jumped back in the truck. We said our goodbyes, and they drove off to check out the next location on their list.

It was getting into late afternoon, and if Laura was going to leave, it was time for her to go. I helped her with her suitcase, and we loaded up her car. We held each other in the driveway for a long time before she went.

"You take care of my babies," she instructed, talking about Oscar, Peaches, and Squatchie.

Then she headed out, driving down Altruria and coming out at the entrance at Bicentennial, where we had first walked up. She didn't encounter any police on the way down, and the guards at the gate let her drive out without any trouble.

As she left, she passed by convoys of troops being brought in by the national guard. They were not taking their duties lightly and had mobilized huge numbers of soldiers to protect the neighborhoods. They began to set up checkpoints every few blocks, and by morning there would be three sets of soldiers within shouting distance of the entrance to Viewpointe Circle. Unlike the police, they weren't just going to drive by every now and then. They had come to occupy the disaster zones and would hold their positions day and night until told to stand down.

Laura was planning to stay in Petaluma with the parents of our landlord. They had offered her a spare bedroom and made her a home-cooked meal when she arrived. She texted me later that the hot shower was heavenly.

Back at the circle, we got ready for dinner. Hot dogs and beer again!

I had begun to understand what Oscar felt like, always eating the same kibble for his meals.

This was the day when Dave asked to pet Oscar. I showed him how to hold out his hand to be sniffed, and the two met. Oscar looked up at Dave, his ears back and the stump of his tail wagging, and Dave looked down, stroking Oscar's head gently. The two of them were an interesting pair. The retired firefighter, who thought that he would never have another chance to do the work he loved, and the working dog who I never thought would get a chance to do the job he was bred for. The fire gave a second chance to one and a first chance to the other. It was the intersection of old and new, and the two of them had been perfect candidates for the jobs they had been given: you couldn't ask for a better Chief than Dave, and you couldn't ask for a better watchdog than Oscar.

As we were sitting down, and after I had taken Oscar home, a man wearing spandex on a fancy white road bike pulled into the circle and rode past us slowly. He was an older guy and had gray hair. Sebastian and I were up out of our chairs immediately and started walking toward him.

"What are you doing here?" Sebastian asked him in a loud voice.

"What are YOU doing here?" he responded sarcastically. It was obvious that he didn't like being challenged.

I don't think he realized that he had ridden into a circle. When he got to the bend and realized that he couldn't just ride away from us, he turned around and headed back.

"We live here. We've been here since the beginning," Gary said back to him. Gary had come into the street as well.

"You don't belong here," Dave shouted at the cyclist. He hadn't gotten up but was watching all of us from his place at the table.

The cyclist rode past Sebastian and me, back the way he had come. I had the urge to block his path but didn't. We turned to follow him.

"I've been here since the beginning, too," he said. He knew he was outnumbered, and we weren't going to back down. He was heading for the entrance, but his ego forced him to mouth off at us the whole way.

"You look pretty clean!" Gary shouted after him. It was true. Had he been living in the neighborhood the whole time like we had, he'd look more like us. Being covered in soot and only having access to cold showers gives one a certain well-worn look that you don't have when coming from the outside world.

Although the cyclist had a total attitude problem, we didn't think he was a looter. He didn't have a backpack, and there was no way for him to carry any loot. He was just some guy that thought it would be fun to take a bike ride through the evacuation zone. I don't think he realized how close he came to being pushed off his bike and held down until the police arrived.

Once he left, we returned to the table and discussed whether or not to call the cops and give the cyclist some trouble. I had my phone out and was ready to do it, but Dave talked me down. The police had better things to do with their time than harass some crotchety old guy on a bike. He wouldn't be coming back this way again, despite all his bluster.

The Pliny was finished off, and we made a dent in our "regular" beer supply as well. Eddie did make it back to his DJ booth for a second round of music, but things got nowhere near the crazy levels of the previous night. Most of us turned in relatively early.

As I got ready for bed, I heard a series of texts come in. The neighborhood was saying goodnight.

### #VIEWPOINTE STRONG

**EDDIE:** Good night from Pointe Patrol. All is good in the hood!

**BONNIE:** 😴 sweet dreams team thank you again

**ELLIOT:** Good night gang

**DENISE:** Good night!!! 🙏❤️🙏

That night, as I lay there in bed, I found myself thinking about Laura and TJ, the missing members of the tribe. It felt different without them.

I also reflected on how sweet it was that the neighbors always texted to say goodnight to each other.

I realized that where you belong has nothing to do with the home you own. It has everything to do with the people around you. Half of us were renters. We weren't even fighting for our own properties. What we were fighting for was our community: the chance to see Hunter riding his bike in the street with Wayne at his side; the ability for Peaches and Benny to interact, and for Elaine and us to be entertained and touched by their strange friendship; for the goofy monthly potlucks that we all attended.

I didn't need to own a home again to find my place. Putting down roots didn't have anything to do with buying a house. What I needed was to be around people whom I cared about and who cared about me. I found that at Pointe Patrol. Home was a couple plastic tables in front of Eddie's garage. That was enough; nothing more was required. If there was ever a root put down anywhere, I sure put one down in those two weeks. It was a strong root, and one that ran deep, like the roots of the massive oaks that survived the fire in the area behind our house. Sometimes tumbleweeds get lucky and get to stop rolling, and sometimes fires do more than destroy.

# CHAPTER 14

# Camping out with the National Guard

BONNIE WAS THE first to send a text the next morning. Pointe Patrol had already been up and about when it came through.

**#VIEWPOINTE STRONG**

> **BONNIE:** Good morning Pointe Patrol. Outliers checking in wanting to see how you guys were doing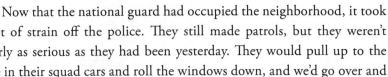
>
> **ME:** We're doing well. Friendly cops today.

Now that the national guard had occupied the neighborhood, it took a lot of strain off the police. They still made patrols, but they weren't nearly as serious as they had been yesterday. They would pull up to the café in their squad cars and roll the windows down, and we'd go over and chat with them. Their lives had become simpler. Ours had, too. We were now confined to just the circle itself, but we were happy to trade that for the blanket of protection that the national guard provided.

**BONNIE:** So Shawn will be bringing ice by at some point today. Bless his wonderful heart. How are you guys doing on food?

Shawn had become a regular visitor to the circle, and the neighborhood had officially adopted him. He would spend his nights with the outside group at the hotel, and then he'd come and visit us during the day as he made his rounds for work. He always came bearing gifts.

We were short on food, and people began to chime in about the supplies we needed. One of the key provisions that we had to manage was our gas. We needed to leave the generator running to keep our food refrigerated, and it was important to keep an eye on the gas supply to do that.

Wayne was planning to do a gas run for us, while Bonnie and Ted would gather the food. Finding someone to deliver it up to us was an issue, but that didn't seem like an insurmountable problem.

We didn't need ice, though. Shawn loved bringing it to us, but there was nowhere to put it. As far as beer, even though we had gone through the Pliny, we still had enough other kinds to stock a bar. There was more beer than food.

**ME:** No more ice for a while.

**ME:** No more beer either. We're overflowing with beer and ice at this point

**TED:**

**BONNIE:**

Shortly after we all finished breakfast and cleaned up, TJ returned. Between Viewpointe Circle and the Gardenview group, there were three police officers that lived in the neighborhood. TJ had made it back up with one of them. The police were following two different scripts. On one hand, there were the official rules, which stated that there was an evacuation zone and that no one was supposed to be going up into it. But on the other hand, the police were people, and they wanted to do the right thing. TJ wasn't a looter and had risked his life to keep the neighborhood safe. Everyone knew this. The bureaucrats might make the rules, but cops on the ground were the ones that had to enforce them, and they wanted to do their part to make things better, not worse.

When TJ showed up, we all gave him big hugs and welcomed him back. He had used his outside time wisely and had taken a number of hot showers. The rest of us were jealous.

"Dude, you totally got profiled," someone told TJ after we had all greeted him.

"I know! That guy just wouldn't listen," he agreed.

"You went out there dressed all ghetto with your flat-brimmed hat. And a backpack—just like a looter! What did you think would happen?" Wayne asked, laughing.

"We need to teach you how to walk like a white guy," one of us offered.

"Do it like this," Gary suggested and then started walking down the sidewalk. He walked very straight and stiff. TJ followed behind him, mimicking how Gary was walking.

"Pretend like you've got a stick up your butt, TJ. You've got too much swagger," I offered.

"I can't walk like that, man," TJ replied.

"He's too cool to walk like a white guy. It's in his blood," Eddie said. We all laughed. It was good to have TJ back. It felt like an injustice had been righted.

Wayne was never able to spend much time with us at once during the day. He would only pop in now and then for a few minutes when he was in the area, and then he'd take off. He was still extremely busy, and it was time for him to go again. He drove partway off and then stopped, rolling down his window and leaning out toward us.

"I love you fuckers," he said to the group of us that were standing there. As far as intimate exchanges went, I suspected that this was about as much emotion as Wayne was willing or able to display to a bunch of his buddies.

"We love you, too, Wayne," I said back to him. He smiled and then drove off.

Shortly before noon, a team from Comcast showed up and double-checked the connections in the neighborhood. They told us we would have internet as soon as power came back on. The utility crew appeared after they had left. This was good news.

> **SEBASTIAN:** PGE crew on Viewpointe, they are hopeful power may be restored by end of day
>
> **ELLIOT:** Yeah!!!
>
> **NICOLE:** Give them some of the extra beer!!!
>
> **DOTTIE:** HUGE
>
> **BONNIE:** Break out the champagne

PG&E spent the next few hours working on the street. We would chat with them when we had the opportunity, but we tried to leave them alone and let them do their work.

At 3 p.m., I heard people cheering. I wasn't sure what had happened, but then I saw Sebastian's text come through.

> **SEBASTIAN:** Power will be back in 10 mins
>
> **SEBASTIAN:** According to PGE crew
>
> **ME:** 😊
>
> **ME:** I was wondering what that cheering was about!
>
> **NORMA:** Woo Hoo! Best news all day!
>
> **NICOLE:** My timer is set and counting
>
> **FOUNTAINVIEW MIKE:** This is Fountainview Mike. If it really comes on please let us know. That would be awesome!

Like Laura, Fountainview Mike had returned to the outside world. Parts of Kaiser had opened back up, and he could only put his patients off for so long. He also had begun to miss his family.

At 2:56, power came back.

**SEBASTIAN:** We got power!!!!

**ME:** Power is up!!!

**BONNIE:** OMG!!!!!

**MIKE:** Awesome!!

**EDDIE:** We got the power! VIEWPOINTE STRONG BABY!

Needless to say, we were all thrilled. We had been without power for seven days.

**LAURA:** Do not forget to close fridge doors, guys.

Laura made a good point. The power had gone out the night everyone evacuated, and we had made a point to prop all the refrigerator doors open. Now that the power was back on, there was some work to do.

**MIKE:** Definitely going to have to get my key up there! My fridge is open

**ME:** I'm gonna close all the fridges I can now

As I stepped out of my house, I heard alarms wailing. They were coming from the Boulders, and they were loud.

**ME:** All the alarms at the apartments are going off now. Lol

The PG&E crew realized that the alarms going off would be completely irritating to us, and so they shut the power back off to the Boulders. No one was there to turn any of those alarms off, so they would hold off on restoring power until management could show up and help handle the situation.

A group of us met at the café, ready to go around and close all the open refrigerators. It was decided that we would also turn off any lights that were on inside people's houses but would leave both the front and backyard lights on.

The way I thought we should approach this was to divide the keys among all the people present and have everyone do three or four houses. That way, by working together, we could complete the entire street in less than an hour. Chief had other plans. He wanted to do one house at a time, and he wanted to be personally present to double-check each one.

That was probably the most inefficient way of doing the task, and the result was that Chief got to do most of the houses himself. Gary and I helped with a few, but after a while we found other jobs to do rather than wait around to try to talk another key out of the Key Master.

I checked my phone and saw that Eddie had sent something to the thread.

**EDDIE:**

**EDDIE:** You done good.

He was right. That generator had made a huge difference. Things would have been a lot harder without it. I helped Eddie pack it up onto a dolly, and we wheeled it over to Joe and Carmen's house, where we stashed it in the garage.

I returned home and did a little work for my job. I was able to get online and answer a few emails. My brain wasn't in the right place to do anything serious, so I just dipped my toes in the water and tried to do what I could. As I was working, I noticed that both the cats were sitting on the windowsill in the kitchen, looking intently at something off to the right. Oscar came up and followed their gaze. He started growling.

I made my way over to see what they were all looking at. It was Joe. He was climbing over the edge of the railing on his back deck. I'm not sure what he had been up to in his backyard, but I chuckled to myself as I saw him haul himself up onto his deck. I texted Pointe Patrol.

### Pointe Patrol

**ME:** Joe is looting his own house. Oscar caught him

**LAURA:** Carmen will return to an empty wine cooler

Joe had come up to turn his lights off and close his refrigerator doors. He had driven himself up, without an escort. Somehow, he had managed to talk his way past all the sentries that had secured the area. He was pretty amazing in that regard. It wasn't the first time he had been able to simply show up when everyone else had been blocked.

That night, as usual, we had hot dogs and beer for dinner. It had become a ritual to get some music playing for dinner, and Eddie didn't disappoint, firing up his DJ equipment. He even played some old-fashioned music for Dave. This was the first night that I had come to dinner without my flashlight. The whole street was lit up but completely quiet aside from us. Everything looked perfect. It felt like we were on a movie set.

Sebastian posted a picture of Eddie with his headphones on at the DJ booth.

### #VIEWPOINTE STRONG

**SEBASTIAN:** Friday... Monday... doesn't matter. Whiskey + street lights party!
**WAYNE:**

It was almost 10 a.m. the next morning before anything came through on the text thread.

**NORMA:** Good Morning Pointe Patrol! Thinking that you all had a good night since I am not seeing updates this morning. Can't thank you enough for all you've done for our hood. Max and Libby can't wait to give you some doggie kisses.
**ME:** 😊

Norma was right, things had settled down considerably. No one did night patrols anymore. The national guard maintained their positions twenty-four hours a day, so if anything happened, they'd be there to deal with it. Now that we had power back, some of us had started doing some work during the day. Eddie and Gary would both disappear for hours to work on their computers. I spent my share of time answering emails as well. I wasn't quite ready to think about watching television yet—I didn't need any more drama in my life than what was already there—but I know that wasn't true for everyone else.

I still took Oscar around the circle frequently. It gave us both something to do, and keeping an eye on the neighborhood was never a bad idea. The national guard was watching it from the outside, and we would watch it from the inside.

On one of my patrols, I saw Dave walking with his box of keys. He was still making the rounds, double-checking people's inside lights and closing their fridges. He brought an orange bucket with him and would leave it in front of whatever house he was working on. That way, if any of us needed to find him, all we had to do was look for the bucket. He had a beer with him and was taking his time, making sure to do a good job. It wasn't work for him. I think he was really enjoying himself. Like Oscar, he had a purpose, and that wasn't something he felt like giving up just yet.

> **TED:** Group: I sent a note to Wayne earlier about dinner items for tonight... haven't heard but I'm sure he's busy! I'll take dinner suggestions from anyone and we can figure out a way to get it up to you... no rush

This was the biggest issue of the day: what to have for dinner. We were running low on supplies.

> **WAYNE:** I'll get dinner to them if you can make a meet. Bonnie knows the drill

> **SEBASTIAN:** TJ says pizza, I second that if possible.

The last thing anyone at Pointe Patrol was going to suggest was a resupply of our hot dog stores. It was time for something else.

**ME:** I was thinking the same thing!!!

**ME:** I bet we could get delivery to the MPs and I could pick up from there

**EDDIE:** +4

**SEBASTIAN:** They can use a drone for the drop off

**BONNIE:** 👏

**ME:** lol. If a hummer drives in here with a pizza, don't forget to take a pic!

The national guard had been taking pretty good care of us. Having them do a pizza run for us was strangely not as far out of the realm of possibility as it should have been.

**EDDIE:** Sushi?

**ME:** Ok that would be awesome too

**BONNIE:** If Dave isn't paying attention to this thread at the moment he adores sushi

We had just upped the ante from hot dogs to pizza to sushi. It was going to be a good day. Too bad we were out of Pliny.

**EDDIE:** What would the Viewpointe roll be?

**ME:** Burned shrimp with lots of wasabi

**BONNIE:** I believe there is such a thing as a firecracker roll

**TED:** I'll need time to pull this together... Pizza and sushi?

**ME:** If that's what we're having for dinner, things are officially settled down. Just saying

I felt that if we had enough time and energy to be debating dinner to this extent, it showed that the neighborhood was in a good position. It would make Ted's job a little more difficult, but Dave kept his house from burning down, so I think he was willing to jump through a few hoops for us in exchange.

**EDDIE:** TJ wants Buffalo wings with sauce

**BONNIE:** Dave doesn't like hot spicy

**EDDIE:** Put it on the side?

Now things were starting to get a little out of hand.

**WAYNE:** If it's not too much trouble I would like a 3 course meal... catered... with a bottle of wine and I could really use a massage.

**BONNIE:**

In the end, I think it was clear that we were just going crazy and wouldn't stop suggesting different kinds of food until dinner had come. Ted knew this and chose to focus on pizza, which was a good decision on his part. Otherwise we'd have had him running all over town on an endless quest for delicacies.

It was late afternoon when Fountainview Mike texted. There was a downed pole up on Fountainview, so his street still hadn't gotten power back.

**FOUNTAINVIEW MIKE:** Hi all. Fountainview Mike here. Hoping to go to my house for a few. Are they letting people walk or drive in?

**ELLIOT:** No

**ME:** Depends on if they like you. Bring your ID

**ELLIOT:** We tried just earlier and were stopped 3 times

**FOUNTAINVIEW MIKE:** I will bring my ID and cookies to bribe the gate keeper 🙂

**ELLIOT:** Good luck 👍

Fountainview Mike did eventually make it up that day, but not by driving up himself. Only Joe was slick enough to be able to pull something like that off. Mike came up the way everyone else did—by getting a ride from one of the three cops that lived in the area.

We had another interesting visitor that afternoon. A pickup truck pulled up right outside the café as a group of us were sitting there. Two men stepped out. One was wearing a reflective yellow firefighter's jacket and had what almost looked like a backpack that he wore on his front. He had handheld radios attached to it and a bunch of other gear stuffed in the pockets. This was the Branch 3 fire director, who was in charge of managing all the firefighting crews in the area. He had come with his assistant, who was a muscular-looking younger guy.

Both of them talked really fast, and it seemed almost as if they had drunk way too much coffee. Their handshakes were almost too strong. I think they were intense people to begin with, and now they had been thrown into an emergency situation that had them completely amped up. Dave immediately perked up when he found himself face-to-face with his own people.

The fire director heard about us from the many fire trucks that had passed through Viewpointe during the last week, and he wanted to take the opportunity to meet us himself since he was in the area. We told him what we had been up to and gave him a quick blow-by-blow of all the actions we had taken in the days following the evacuation. He nodded approvingly as Dave filled him in on what we had done to prepare that first night.

The conversation took a detour when we told him about what had happened up at the Boulders.

"We called two fire trucks, and both times nobody showed up," one of the guys said. We weren't blaming anyone, as we understood what was going on in the bigger picture, but at the same time we wanted him to know. If the Branch 3 fire director is standing right in front of you, and you've been blown off twice when you called a fire truck for help, odds are that you are going to bring that fact up with the guy. And we did.

He nodded in understanding.

"We didn't have enough firefighters to put out all the fires in the first few days. Our top priority was saving lives," he said, explaining some of the overall strategy that they had been working with.

"That first night was interesting. When the fires hit, we had a lot of units downtown dealing with arson from the homeless population."

A new law had taken effect that allowed police officers to arrest homeless people for misdemeanor offences, such as obstructing the sidewalk with their tents. The police had only been allowed to write tickets up until that point, most of which just ended up getting ripped up in their faces by people who had nothing more to lose and weren't afraid of fines. The new law allowed the police to actually put those people in jail for a night. It was controversial, and many of the homeless didn't like it. The response from some of them was to start fires downtown.

"It wouldn't have mattered from the perspective of saving any structures, but we were a little out of position when the fires came through because of that.

"Then we had to deal with Kaiser. That took up a lot of resources."

Kaiser had been evacuated that first night. I had watched footage of it at Judith's, where they showed nurses and doctors pushing sick people out of the hospital on wheeled beds, smoke and flames in the background.

"I had an argument with the head doctor," he continued. "I told him 'We can definitely hold this line. I guarantee that we can keep the hospital from burning. You don't need to evacuate.'

"His response was, 'Smoke is going to get in there, and compromised patients might die. If we don't evacuate right now, their deaths will be on your head.'

"So we evacuated."

At this point, the group split into two conversations, one surrounding the fire director, and another surrounding his assistant, who had been giving us details of what areas had burned and what hadn't. The destruction was vast. Almost everything to the north of us was gone. I moved back and forth between the two conversations, interested in what both of these guys had to say.

When I turned my attention back to the fire director, he was giving out his personal cell phone number.

"If you run into any trouble and can't get help, you call me directly. You can call any time, day or night."

I pulled out my phone and added his number to my favorites, so I could access it quickly in an emergency. I couldn't help but laugh when I noticed how my contact list had changed over the last week. It used to be just Laura and my family on there. Now I had police dispatch, Wayne, and the Branch 3 fire director programmed on speed dial, plus over thirty individual contacts for everyone else in the neighborhood, and I could tell you which person lived in each house. Before the fire, my contact list had been a barren desert, but now it felt like the land of milk and honey.

The fire director's assistant interrupted him and reminded him about a meeting he had to make, and the two of them drove off. It was nice of him to stop by, and I was glad that someone like that was in charge of dealing with the fire. He seemed extremely capable.

At 5 p.m., Ted texted an update about the pizzas. He had been giving us regular updates on his status throughout the day: what pizza place he was going to, how far away he was, how long it would take for them to cook the pizzas once he placed the order. That kind of thing. Those of us who had been living on hot dogs for a week were completely glued to those updates.

> **TED:** Got three! Two that will stop your heart and a healthy one!!
>
> **ME:** Excellent. We can save the healthy one for breakfast
>
> **TED:** I think one is called "widowmaker"

Wayne showed up with the pizzas, and we had a feast. It was some of the best pizza I had ever eaten. I'm not sure how it would have compared to my favorite pizza places during regular times, but in that moment, on that day, it was completely amazing.

After dinner, I took Oscar out for his last patrol of the day.

Since TJ had gotten hauled out of the area by the police, we had severely cut back on any excursions outside Viewpointe Circle itself. It was safe on the inside but not so safe on the outside. There was a very clear line that marked the inside of the circle and the outside. Almost every house on the street had its front and back lights on, which made it easy to walk around in the middle of the night without a flashlight. However, none of the street lights had come back on, so everything outside our circle was dark. Because of that, we had the distinct feeling of being in a bubble at night.

I would walk out to the edge of the circle and peer out into the darkness. Even after all this time, it was still surprising how black things were at night. The blackness surrounded us, and there was a natural hesitation to step out into it. I can imagine how our ancestors must have felt staring out into the wilderness at night, wondering what predators lurked there. That feeling can be educated out of us as modern humans, but there's no way to totally get rid of it. Being scared of things that go bump in the night is probably coded into our DNA.

As I stood there on the edge of the circle with Oscar, looking out into the night, I heard a branch crack. My ears perked up, and I held my breath, listening more intently. I heard another muffled sound, and then a third. There was something in the ditch between us and the Boulders.

Had it been a few days earlier, I'd have grabbed my flashlight and gone over to investigate. But now I hesitated. I didn't have my flashlight with me and would have to go back home to get it if I wanted to venture out. I also was concerned about all the national guard in the area. I had been mistaken for a looter enough times in the last week. I didn't want that to happen again if I ended up following sounds that led me away from the circle and into places where I wasn't supposed to be.

As I was pondering my next step, Eddie came up from behind. He was carrying a basket full of wet clothes. He had been doing laundry and was taking a load over to Sebastian's to dry it. The gas was still out, so none of us had dryers that worked except for Sebastian, who had an electric one.

"I think there's something in the ditch," I said to him.

He paused, and the three of us stood there, listening intently to catch sounds of whatever was in the ditch. We didn't hear anything, and we eventually gave up, making our way to Sebastian's.

"Dude, tell the national guard. Let them chase down whoever is out there," Eddie suggested. He was right—it wasn't my job to have to chase looters off anymore. That's why they were here.

Sebastian opened the door and welcomed us. He was watching TV, and the Warriors game was on. He invited us in to join him. Eddie was more than happy to accept, but I declined, still concerned about what I had heard. I wasn't sure if Sebastian would want Oscar running around his house either, and I didn't want to impose.

Instead of joining them inside, I went around to the backyard, which was just above Altruria. The national guard had been posted just behind his house. I looked down and couldn't see anything. There were no lights on where they had been earlier.

"Hey! Are you still down there?" I called out toward the area where I remembered them being stationed.

There was a moment's silence, and then a woman's voice answered.

"Yes, we're here!" The national guard hadn't left for the night. They were sitting at their posts in the dark. That would make for an unpleasant surprise for some looter sneaking around in the dark.

"I heard something in the ditch by the apartments. There were looters over there the other day... " I explained. Wayne and Gary and a couple other guys had seen flashlights at the Boulders a couple nights back and had gone running after them. Unfortunately, not being completely strategic about how it had been done, some of our guys had turned their flashlights on as they ran. When the looters saw lights coming their way, their flashlights went out, and they split. Wayne had poked fun at our side's lack of tactics after that.

"You've got to sneak up on them in the dark and then turn your flashlights on right as you surprise them," he had said the next morning, imitating attacking someone with his elbow. We had all gotten a kick out of the story, but the fact that strange people were still roaming around in the night had reminded us that we weren't completely out of the woods yet. We wouldn't be until the evacuation had been lifted and everyone had returned home. As long as there were evacuated houses in the area, looters would be trying to figure out how to get in.

I heard some murmuring from the national guard but couldn't see what they were doing. I made my way back to the entrance to the circle and stopped, watching. I heard some guards across the street but couldn't see them. They had walked up in the dark and weren't using flashlights. Like Wayne, they didn't want to give away their position before they knew what they were dealing with. I probably didn't help with that as I called out to them.

"It was right there in that ditch. It leads all the way up this street. Someone could sneak in all the way by just following that. There were some looters in the area a couple nights ago, and maybe they're trying to come back," I said.

"Thank you, sir."

I could see the guards now, and they turned their flashlights on as they peered into the ditch. They were dressed in camouflage and had pistols in holsters at their sides. They were peering down into the creek, trying to see what was down there. The bushes made it difficult.

One of the guards moved down into the ditch and slipped as he got to the steep part. He fell on his rear, and then quickly got back up and continued down. His partner joined him, helping scan the area. I watched a little longer and figured there was nothing left to do, so I turned to go home.

I texted an update to Pointe Patrol as I walked.

### Pointe Patrol

**ME:** MPs are working their way up that ditch. I hope I didn't send them on a wild goose chase

**EDDIE:** Better to be safe than sorry. Good lookin out!

**ME:** There are acorns and there is creeping and this sounded like creeping

**EDDIE:** I am chillin at Sebastian's house for a minute watching the Warriors game. He is drying my laundry in his drier!

**ME:** Laundromat is open for business!

**LAURA:** Lol. Did Lisa stay?

Lisa is Sebastian's girlfriend. She had been up to the circle a couple times in the last week but hadn't stayed. She originally wanted to, but Sebastian felt that he wouldn't be able to do any work because he'd be worrying about her too much. But now that power was back, she had come home.

**ME:** Yes

**LAURA:** Good!!!!

**ME:** Wayne told Sebastian to put a ring on it

**LAURA:** I agree! I told Sebastian as much.

**EDDIE:** It's got to be in the circle

I was momentarily surprised to see Eddie chime in. For some reason, I thought I had been on a private text with Laura, but we were still on the Pointe Patrol thread. So much for Sebastian's relationship privacy!

**ME:** Lisa told us to put pressure on him. It's year 5

**SEBASTIAN:** First let's talk about the bachelor party!

**LAURA:** He'll do it after this. I have no doubt.

**ME:** Lol. We could have an awesome one

**LAURA:** Dude, you just got a 10-day bachelor party.

**EDDIE:** Sebastian is on fire!

**EDDIE:** Oops did I just say that?

**ME:** Lol

**SEBASTIAN:** Yea, but it would be better if I could at least take a hot shower

**EDDIE:** No buckets necessary

# CHAPTER 15

# Lifting the Evacuation

THE NEXT MORNING, Laura had some great news that she posted to the big thread.

### #VIEWPOINTE STRONG

**LAURA:** Hey everyone, the national guard just told me Viewpointe Circle can come and go with ease with passes!!!!!

This set off a flurry of texts from the neighborhood.

**BONNIE:** Why who. Are those passes we pick up? And does that mean we can actually live in our homes??

**SEBASTIAN:** What passes??

**DOTTIE:** Do you know where we get passes?

**BONNIE:** I'm looking for that information now give me a minute

**LAURA:** 😊😊😊

This was great news. It was time for people to come home. It sounded like the authorities were working on a way to make that happen.

Rather than the usual police patrols through the neighborhood, today we had tan Humvees visit, driven by military police. We smiled and waved from the café as one of the Humvees made a lap around Viewpointe Circle. Wayne took a picture and posted it to the thread.

The national guard had very strict rules about accepting any food or gifts from people. They were here to help, and from their perspective, that meant not reducing the provisions of the people they were trying to protect. So no matter how many times we offered them a cup of coffee, they always politely refused. Wayne understood what was going on and decided to find a loophole.

"They're up here 24/7 guarding our shit. We need to give them some coffee," he said, his mind made up. We had more than enough coffee to go around, so he made a few cups and walked out of the circle with them, heading up Altruria to the closest group of soldiers.

A few minutes later, he came back, no longer holding the coffee. He had a huge smile on his face.

"They can't accept food from civilians, but I'm not a civilian. I'm with the sheriff's department. It's OK for them to take coffee from me."

Bonnie had an update about the passes.

> **BONNIE:** We do not need passes. You do need your valid ID that shows the address on Viewpointe Circle. And I'm pretty sure this applies to Mike and Sheri up on Fountainview too
>
> **BONNIE:** And mind this is under the radar folks under the radar please keep it that way
>
> **BONNIE:** The only access is through Lake Park and Terralinda
>
> **LAURA:** Yes, that's true. I just got off the phone with the city and they say NG has misleading info. BUT, if you go to Terralinda and Lake Park, you will get winked ;) through. That said, I really do encourage everyone to return to your home for at least a few hours today.

Ted had an update about the passes. Bonnie had posted more than we had seen but accidentally sent the information to an older thread that was no longer active, and almost no one had gotten that part of her message.

> **TED:** I'm going to post Bonnie's text from the other thread starting right now: OK I'm going to make this as concise as possible.
>
> **TED:** This is under the radar. Exclamation exclamation exclamation I cannot emphasize this enough. You do not. Do not spread this information to friends and family other than those of us in our neighborhood!!!!
>
> **TED:** I just got off the phone with SRPD lieutenant. Number one most important most important most important
>
> **LAURA:** Yes, do not let the Eye of Sauron see you!!
>
> **MIKE:** Got it!!
>
> **TED:** Please adhere to "tell no one" or we lose our privileges

What it felt like to me was that the city wasn't ready to open up all the evacuation zones yet, but at the same time they didn't want to keep people out of neighborhoods that were still standing. The big issue was that the search and rescue team hadn't yet been able to identify the remains of everyone who had perished in the fires, and they didn't want to let people back into those areas until that process had been completed.

Weeks later, I came across someone who had been involved in that work. He said that it was incredibly difficult to identify remains in a situation like this, since they were almost completely incinerated by the heat. A lot of times it came down to finding something like a titanium knee replacement and tracking that back to the victim who had undergone surgery for it. The last thing the city wanted to happen was for a family to go back to their destroyed home, and for them to be the ones to stumble across the remains of a loved one.

Wayne interrupted the conversation with a picture. He had secured a set of #VIEWPOINTE STRONG flags for our yards.

**WAYNE:**

**WAYNE:** The owner of this company's son lives in the Boulders Apts. When I went to pay for our banners he started asking questions. After sharing our story he gave them to us. Give this guy love, posts, likes, whatever other nerdy computer stuff I don't know about. Help do this guy a SOLID!!!

**WAYNE:** Small business owner in our community with a big heart 🖤

Wayne's plan was to get some stakes and put one of these banners in every yard on Viewpointe Circle, except for Mr. Difficult's. Mr. Difficult wasn't getting a banner.

Various neighbors began to show up that day. Norma made it up first, then Elliot, and others as well. The national guard had a map of the area, and if we could prove that we lived in a house that hadn't burned down, they would let us drive up. The curfew was still in effect, and we weren't supposed to cruise around and see the sights, but those were conditions people were gladly willing to accept. Laura and I had printed out our lease agreement for our house and kept copies in our cars to prove where we lived. I never actually had to use that, or even show my ID coming in and out. I was practically on a first-name basis with the guards in the area, so they recognized me on sight and let me through whenever I came and went over the next week.

Laura came home, too. Unlike the others, she had come to stay. She had been busy in her time away and showed up with two black garbage bags full of clean laundry. She had taken advantage of being in a house with gas and electric and gotten us some clean clothes. I was getting pretty low on socks and underwear, so that was a nice surprise.

I was happy to see her again, but Oscar was ecstatic. He knows not to jump on people, and he got around that rule on this occasion by practicing his *fly-bys* in his excitement, repeatedly jumping through the air just past Laura, his head right at eye level, his tongue darting out in an attempt to kiss her nose.

When Joe and Carmen came up, they brought some groceries for us, and of course that meant we now had a full supply of hot dogs and buns for dinner. As we were getting ready to start cooking them, we were interrupted by a white truck that pulled up to the café. It was the Red Cross. Their truck had a window on the side that could slide open, and there was a team of volunteers inside from all over the country.

"How would you all like a hot dinner, cooked by the Southern Baptists?" one of them asked us, as we stood around their truck in a semi-circle, like a bunch of little kids surrounding an ice cream truck. We happily agreed, and food and supplies began flowing into the café. They wanted to give us water and ice, too, but we didn't need either.

They gave us containers with warm, cooked food inside. We had meatloaf, mashed potatoes, green beans, salad, fruit, and a bun. It was perfect.

"Where's the pudding?" Laura asked in jest, and they all laughed.

The Red Cross had a simple mission: they were going to drive around the evacuation areas, and they were going to give food to whomever they could find. It doesn't sound like anything glamorous. They weren't eradicating a deadly disease or saving lives. They were just feeding people. But being the person on the receiving end of that gesture, it made a deep impact on me. In that moment, I became a huge fan of the Red Cross and vowed to help their cause as soon as things returned to normal.

The volunteers were amazing and had come from as far away as Tennessee and Ohio. They had piled into their truck and driven out to California so that they could find us and give us dinner. It meant a lot that they were willing to help out in that way, and we were all touched by their compassion.

Over the next week or two, once people started coming back to the area to sort through what was left of their homes, that truck would make its way through the neighborhoods and try to find people to feed. I could hear them broadcasting through a megaphone as they slowly made their way from neighborhood to neighborhood, saying, "This is the Red Cross. We have warm food and clean water."

The next morning, two PG&E trucks showed up. They were ready to turn the gas back on but had to go house by house to do it. Dave sent out a text to the group with the news.

## #VIEWPOINTE STRONG

**DAVE:** To all. PGE gas is here to start restoring gas service to all homes we have key access to.

**TED:** 🙂

**NORMA:** Best news of the day!

It was slow going, as pilot lights had to be lit and furnaces tested. The last thing PG&E wanted was to blow up the neighborhood right after we had survived the fire. Since there were two technicians, gas was restored on the block two houses at a time. Dave would unlock the houses and let the technicians in, and the rest of us mostly stood around and cheered them on.

Eddie's house was the first to get gas.

**EDDIE:** Hot water is running here!!!!!

**LAURA:** Omg!!!!!

**ME:** I was so excited about taking a coffee-maker hot water sponge bath today. This is so much better!

I was only half-joking. I had actually planned to heat up some water with our coffee maker and use that for a sponge bath. I was ready to try anything to avoid having to take another cold shower.

Getting gas back was a huge deal. It was the last thing left to restore before the neighborhood was back to its original state, as far as that was possible.

As we got closer to noon, our friends in the Red Cross truck returned. They pulled up in front of the café, and everyone was happy to see them.

"Do you all want some lunch?" the driver asked us, starting to pass out food.

"We've got something special for you," one of the Red Cross team members told us, and she handed over a heavy food container. It was a box full of pudding! They had remembered Laura's joke from yesterday and had gone out and found us some chocolate pudding.

**ME:**

**ME:** Laura—Red Cross delivered your pudding just now!!

Laura had been at home when Red Cross had visited, so I took two of the lunches and brought them back to our place. The pudding got stored in Eddie's refrigerator. He had two girls that were going to visit soon. They'd probably get a kick out of that much chocolate pudding.

As gas was restored to someone's house, Dave would post to the thread and let them know.

**DAVE:** Elliot you have gas 🙀🙀🙀🙀

**ME:** Lol. Don't light any matches over there. We'll have to go through this all over again

**ELLIOT:** Damn just ate chili for lunch

Bonnie had some more good news for us.

**BONNIE:** The control of evacuated areas within the city limits has been handed over to the SRPD. I just got off the phone with the lieutenant I've been in contact with for the last few days. And we are no longer evacuated

**BONNIE:** Repeat we are no longer officially evacuated!!!

**ME:** Yay!

**BONNIE:** What this means is that he literally just finished re-drawing the map around every home still standing in our areas

**HELENE:** 🥂 🎉

**NICOLE:** 👏

They were letting us back in. It would be controlled, and we would all have to get special passes and show IDs to get through the blockade, but everyone who had a house standing was welcome to return. The neighborhood would become whole once more.

The first to return were Eddie's two girls. Laura knew they were coming and sent out special instructions to Pointe Patrol.

### Pointe Patrol

**LAURA:** Pointe Patrol: Eddie's girls will be here tonight. NO DRINKING AND NO CUSSIN' Got it?

**EDDIE:** Copy

I wouldn't say that we had become a rowdy crowd, but Laura probably saw things differently after having been gone for a few days. This is what happens when you lock a bunch of guys together in a neighborhood with too much beer and time on their hands. I think we had probably slipped a few steps down the evolutionary ladder.

Now that gas and electricity had been restored, and people were going to be let back into the neighborhood, there was only one thing left to do at our house to return to normalcy. It was time to let the cats out. They had spent most of their days sitting in the windows, and Squatchie would ask to be let out at every opportunity. It hadn't been safe, so he had never been able to talk us into it, but there wasn't much reason to keep him in any longer. Tomorrow would be the day!

Laura sent out a text to the thread. There were a lot of stray cats around, and we didn't want anyone to think that ours were lost and in need of saving.

> **LAURA:** Evening all, we plan to let our cats out tomorrow morning. Please keep an eye out while driving and don't take them to the pound!
>
> **NORMA:** I will advise Max & Libby not to chase them.
>
> **LAURA:** Thanks Norma. Lol
>
> **JOE:** Now who would do something like that???
>
> **LAURA:** Lol!

The first time we had met Joe and Carmen had been because they trapped Squatchie and took him to the pound. We had gotten over it and become quite close to them, but it was still fun to give them some crap about it when the opportunity presented itself.

The next morning, Peaches and Squatchie went out. Not having been outside since the day of the fire, they were quick to take off and go explore. Laura and I took the opportunity to leave as well and headed out to get some coffee. We drove out past the national guard at the Lake Park entrance. There was a huge line of people on the other side of the barrier trying to get in, and almost all of them were being turned away. I wondered how many people in that line were actually looters in disguise, making a last effort in smooth talking their way into the evacuation zone.

There was definitely some culture shock being out in the world again. Just driving around felt a little strange to me. Down here, there were people going about their lives and being busy, and only a short way up the hill we had been living in our bubble. It was an awkward feeling finding myself in the flow again and it hadn't even been two weeks yet. I wondered how people felt after having been out of society for years. It must be completely disorienting when they try to plug back in.

After coffee, we made a trip to the grocery store and stocked up on some food. We had thrown almost everything in our refrigerator away, and it was bare.

When we returned, there was still a line on the other side of the fire gate. People were parked in their cars, waiting on the side of the road. Most of these people probably still weren't sure if their houses had survived. I remember the stress and anxiety I felt on the first day from not knowing whether our house was still there. Had Laura not been such a rule breaker, there was a chance that we'd be in that line as well.

We drove around the edge of the rest of the cars, cutting to the front of the line, and were stopped by the guards standing next to their Humvee. The same guy who had been posted here before was here again, and he smiled as he recognized us. Most of the national guard were young, and it seemed like they were barely out of high school.

"We got something for you at the grocery store," Laura said, handing him a box of freshly baked cookies. By now, all of the rules about not accepting food from civilians had been thrown out the window. The neighbors at Viewpointe Circle had seen to that. Any time one of us drove up, we brought presents for the national guard. No soldier in the area would ever go wanting for coffee or cookies if we had a say in the matter! Laura and I stopped at every checkpoint all the way up the hill, passing out cookies at each one.

As we pulled into Viewpointe, we found that a huge American flag was flying over the entrance. It was probably twenty feet long and was hanging from a wire that had been stretched between two tall redwood trees on either side of the street. Wayne had ordered it and talked the fire department into using one of their trucks with the big extension ladder to hang it for us. Now, whenever anyone drove in or out of the circle, they'd pass right under our giant flag. I heard Wayne talking about getting a flag like this but wasn't sure what I'd think once it was up. Now that I saw it hanging, I liked it a lot.

Peaches was waiting for us when we parked the car. He purred and leaned into me as I stepped out. He is by far the friendliest cat in the neighborhood, and you could always count on a good greeting from him when he saw you.

"Hi, kitten!" I said to him. He was no longer a kitten, but that's what we called them in the beginning, and the habit had stuck. I reached down and stroked him a few times and then looked at my hand. It was black with soot. He probably had been rolling in it. So much for our carpets. They were trashed already, but this would make them even worse.

Even though people could come back and stay for the night if they wanted to, most of the neighborhood chose to remain away. The smell of smoke inside the houses was overwhelming, and the neighborhood needed some serious remediation before things would be anywhere close to how they had been before the fire. We at Pointe Patrol had lost our sense of smell a long time ago, so none of us cared anymore, and dinner was made up of the usual crowd. It would be like this until insurance adjusters were allowed up into the area and the cleaning crews could get activated.

It was cold the next morning, and I had to wear my jacket. Laura, having taken on the mantle of the mama bear during her time at Pointe Patrol, was concerned about the national guard posted outside all night long.

**LAURA:** NG is freezing today. Bring them coffee when you come. There are six guards total (3 sets of 2)

**WAYNE:** I made a pot. I'll hook em up

We always had good breakfasts at the café. Today we had a bunch of bagels and cream cheese that someone donated on one of their visits yesterday. We weren't forced to use the grill to toast things anymore, so we brought out an electric toaster instead. The odds of getting a completely blackened bagel were much lower that way, which was a nice change.

Wayne had gone out and invited the national guards nearby to come and have some coffee and breakfast with us. They didn't want to abandon their posts but agreed to come one at a time. Otherwise they'd be eating cold rations out of a bag. One by one, they'd walk down, and we'd swarm over them trying to get them some warm food.

One of the guards that came down was a pretty young woman from Southern California. We gave her some coffee and were asking her questions as she waited for her bagel to come out of the toaster. TJ seemed smitten and stood close by, making eyes at her.

Wayne noticed what was going on and went over to the two of them. He looked at her last name, which was stitched into the front of her jacket, and said, "TJ, meet Gonzales. Gonzales, meet TJ." He then gestured to the two of them, bringing his hands together. "There! Now you can talk."

He then turned away, smiling mischievously. TJ and Gonzales both went bright red, and she took her bagel and scampered off without saying much more. The rest of us laughed and joked with TJ once she had gone. I thought he took it pretty well once he got over the initial embarrassment.

After breakfast, Wayne sent a text to the thread.

> **WAYNE:** Hey all, just got called into work they need me to do a fingerprint ID on a dead dude. Nobody should be at my house. SHOOT ON SITE (ask questions later)
>
> **BONNIE:** Get 'em, Oscar!!!
>
> **EDDIE:** Got my slingshot armed.
>
> **DAVE:** Have two staple guns to protect Wayne's house. If I'm not around go to Eddie AKA Mr. Staples 😎😎
>
> **EDDIE:** Would someone please disarm Dave? 😳

Everyone was in a good mood, and there was lots of joking on the thread. We were still very alert and aware that looters might still be an issue, but that threat grew smaller as the neighbors spent more and more time back in their homes.

**DAVE:** Dear Eddie, Unless you're nice to me I will go on camera and tell the world about the Mr. Staples story 😡

**EDDIE:** Are you asking me to end my relationship with your ladder?

**KARLA:** I have a ladder if anyone needs one

Karla had no idea what Dave and Eddie were joking about. She thought they actually needed a ladder. It was too complicated for any of us to try to explain over text.

**EDDIE:** 🖕

**DAVE:** FEELING LOVE IN THE AIR

**EDDIE:** 😄

Now that we could all drive out and get our own food again, the logistics of the thread shifted away from supplying Pointe Patrol, and instead people began working out schedules on who was going to bring food to the national guard. Denise offered to bring them pizzas for dinner, and Bonnie scheduled a Starbucks run for the next morning. I'm not sure what the national guard thought of all this attention, but I doubt they were complaining. Protecting a bunch of codependent neighbors can come with some nice perks in the food department.

Later that night, Laura invited the neighbors to breakfast at the café.

**LAURA:** Bagels and coffee tomorrow am at the cafe. Will ping you when it's ready. If you're on this list you are invited!

The next morning, Laura brought over her huge coffee maker to the café and got involved making coffee and bagels for the neighbors. A few of them came and had breakfast with us.

The chairs eventually got arranged into a small circle, and people sat down and talked with each other as they drank their coffee and munched on their bagels. We didn't have enough chairs for everyone, so I gave mine up for one of the women in the neighborhood.

The tone of breakfast was very different with the newcomers present. With Pointe Patrol, there had been a special bond and quiet comradery that accompanied every gathering. There was always a lot of laughing and joking, and an openness that is easy to feel but hard to explain. We were a brotherhood, and Laura had been our den mother. It wasn't like that now. The dynamic had completely changed.

I noticed that there was an inner circle of chairs, and each one was occupied by women from the outside group. The men stood behind the chairs, listening politely, but were completely quiet. The conversation was dominated by just a couple women in the center, who spun what felt like a nonstop stream of anxious chatter out at the rest of us. For me, this breakfast really marked the transition back to being a regular neighborhood again. It was a surreal, bittersweet moment. Our days as a tribe were over.

Later that day, Fountainview Mike sent a picture over the thread. It was him posing in his yard next to the #VIEWPOINTE STRONG banner that Wayne, Eddie, TJ, and Eddie's girls had put up in his yard.

> **FOUNTAINVIEW MIKE:** Hi all. Mike from Fountainview here. We got power and gas today (we were behind you because of a transformer that was incinerated.) Thanks to the Pointe Patrol for adopting me! You guys are the best

> **SHERI:** #ViewpointeStrong and Pointe Patrol ♥🌍 you all are my heroes! Thanks for adopting us and saving our home and neighborhood.

> **EDDIE:** Welcome home from Pointe Patrol!

The day was spent getting the neighborhood back to normal. During the fire, a lot of yard equipment had become communal property. Now we had to put everything back in its rightful place. Hoses and nozzles were the main things that had gotten moved around, but some people were missing garbage cans and propane tanks. I dragged Agnes's umbrella into her backyard from where we had been using it at the café.

The national guard packed up and left that night. Bonnie saw them go.

**BONNIE:** Just as an FYI folks they picked up the national guard a few minutes ago so we are on our own. Altruria is empty

That was it. We were just a neighborhood again.

**ME:** Last chance TJ!! 😜

During dinner, I had been pushing TJ to run up the street and ask for Gonzales's phone number before they packed up and he lost the opportunity forever. I had been completely gun shy about asking pretty girls out when I was younger and could have used someone to help by giving me a nudge at critical moments back then. But despite my best efforts, I wasn't able to talk TJ into making a move. I couldn't resist the opportunity to give him a little slack for that. Neither could Wayne.

**WAYNE:** (.)(.)

**WAYNE:** 👉 👌

**EDDIE:** Oh dang

I was at home by this point, but Wayne and a bunch of the guys were doing their best to finish off the rest of the beer we had stored at the café. You could tell by the texts that they were all pretty far along.

**WAYNE:** Or in TJ's case 👉👈

I don't know what it was, but Wayne's texts had been the funniest I'd seen in a really long time. I couldn't stop laughing after reading through them. I'll admit, it was grade-school humor, but that's the level most of us were at during those days. Laura didn't totally approve of putting this on the big thread.

**LAURA:** Keep it clean guys, jeez

**TED:** Ditto Laura...

**KARLA:** 😂😂 I just got it. I'm a little slow

**EDDIE:** Time to evacuate

**LAURA:** Eddie, don't say that! Those are sacred words. Hey, Pointe Patrol should revolve into a garage boy band.

Eventually, the neighbors all came back. The neighborhood was awash with insurance adjusters and cleaning people for months. We had gone from a wasteland to what felt like a construction zone. There was no end to the vans and trucks that swarmed over the neighborhood, scrubbing and cleaning the soot and smoke off the houses and everyone's belongings. It only takes fifteen minutes for a house to burn to its foundation, but reversing that process takes months and years depending on the level of damage. We had our neighborhood back, but it was not the same neighborhood that it had been before. It wouldn't be for a long time to come.

The final numbers for the fire were staggering. The Northern California Firestorm was comprised of a series of 250 wildfires that burned over 245,000 acres. They cost at least $9.4 billion in insured damages and were predicted to cost the US economy $85 billion. The fires forced 90,000 people to evacuate their homes and killed forty-four people. Collectively, this event constitutes the largest loss of life due to wildfires in the United States since 1918, and an estimated 8,900 structures were destroyed. Of all those 250 fires that sprung up, it was the Tubbs Fire that broke the record for being the single most destructive fire in California history, accounting for half of the deaths and $1.2 billion of the losses.

It took more than 10,000 firefighters to battle the fires, with more than 1,000 fire engines and associated equipment. Fire crews flew in from as far away as Canada and Australia to assist. According to PG&E, more than 350,000 customers lost electric service, and over 42,000 lost gas during the event.

Various newspapers and magazines heard about what we had done at Viewpointe Circle and wanted our story. For the most part, no one really wanted to tell it to them. It was still too raw, and in those days, we didn't want to talk about how great our neighborhood was when only a block away people had lost everything. It seemed somehow disrespectful to them and what they had been though. But inspiring stories deserve to be told, and eventually we all began to lighten up about telling people what had happened.

Wayne was the first to show up with a journalist from a magazine who wanted to do an article about Pointe Patrol for their next edition.

He broke the news to us via our emergency Pointe Patrol thread, sort of informing us and asking for our blessings at the same time.

> **WAYNE:** Hey gang, I was contacted by a magazine editor and they want to do a story for their next issue. They heard "I" did amazing things 😆. I told the lady there is no "I" in team. Chief shut the fuck up! I know what you are thinking... The roots of our story started long before the fire and we are a role model neighborhood that others can strive to replicate. Life will go on but each of you are TRUE HEROES who put your personal shit on hold to do the right thing.

> **DAVE:** The CHIEF knows nothing! Except that he was part of a team. No more, no less 😁

> **WAYNE:** Chief you motherfucker I wouldn't be in my home giving Hunter a bath if it wasn't for a dumbass like you

> **WAYNE:** Respectfully

Everyone quickly got on board with him doing the interview and gave him our support. We could tell Wayne was feeling exceptionally affectionate toward us all since he was trying hard to squeeze as much cussing as he could into his texts.

> **LAURA:** Wayne, I am delighted that you are such a bright light in the world 🌈

> **TJ:** Rainbows for Wayne!! 🌈🌈🌈🌈

> **WAYNE:** Laura, I just threw up in my mouth

Yes, this was the Pointe Patrol I remembered. I had been missing the back-and-forth that we used to have during the days of the evacuation.

> **ME:** Haha. You know you like it 😜

> **WAYNE:** LIBTARDS

> **EDDIE:** Do I see smolders?

> **EDDIE:** Piss boy?

> **LAURA:** I do hope that you tell them that Dave wanted to kiss Sebastian on the lips. I love that one...

This would be the final exchange we all had as part of Pointe Patrol. It was an honor and a privilege to be a member of that group of heroes. They had been my neighbors, but they had become my family. In his own special way, I think Wayne might have said it the best: I love you fuckers.

#VIEWPOINTE STRONG

# A FEW PICTURES

This is the SUV that was parked across the street from Judith's house in
Graton. Someone had driven it through flames to escape. The headlights
had melted in the heat.

When we returned to our house, the fence was still on fire. This was the last remaining section of it. All the rest had burned.

We came across this car on Fountainview, one street up from us. The wheels had liquefied in the high temperatures and flowed into the street.

This is all that was left of the house on the corner. It only took fifteen minutes for it to burn to its foundations. The devastated Miramonte neighborhood can be seen below.

Pudding delivery! I love the Red Cross.

Oscar and I are ready to go on patrol. Get 'em, Oscar!

I took this picture just down the street from Viewpointe Circle, on the way to the Baldwin gate. Someone had spray-painted "Looters shot onsite" in the street.

This is the flag that Wayne talked the fire department into hanging for us at the entrance to Viewpointe Circle in the weeks following the fire.

# HEY! DID YOU LIKE THIS BOOK?

I'm not a famous author. I'm just some guy that happened to be in the right (wrong?) place last year, and am trying to tell other people about one of the biggest events in my life, as well as in the lives of countless others. I don't have any marketing teams, publicists, or agents. It's just me, and my advertising budget is made up of whatever I was able to scrape together on the side. This book will live or die by word of mouth from readers like you. If you enjoyed reading it, would it be too much if I asked you for an Amazon review? It's easy, you can do it in five minutes, and you'll be playing a not-insignificant role in helping to both spread the word about Pointe Patrol, as well as get my writing career up and running. Seriously, it's a *really* big deal.

If you're willing to help, here's exactly how:

Go to www.amazon.com

In the search bar at the top, type "Pointe Patrol" and scroll down until you recognize this book's cover. Click on it.

Once you're on this book's page, scroll down. You're looking for the *Customer Reviews* section, which is toward the bottom.

When you locate the review section, look for the button that says "Write a customer review." It's gray and is placed at the top of that category, just to the right. Click it!

I really appreciate it. If you took the time to support this book, and we ever run into each other downtown, the Pliny is on me. ☺

# ABOUT THE AUTHOR

Earik Beann is a serial entrepreneur, and over the years he has been involved in many businesses, including software development, an online vitamin store, specialty pet products, a commodity pool, and a publishing house. Before *Pointe Patrol*, he wrote six technical books on esoteric subjects related to financial markets. His original love has always been writing, and one of the silver linings in working on this memoir in the aftermath of the Tubbs Fire was the rekindling of his love of writing simply for the sake of writing. *Killing Adam*, his first science fiction novel, is due to be released in early 2019. He lives in California with his wife Laura, their Doberman, and two Tennessee barn cats.

Please visit Earik's website to learn more about his books, and join his newsletter to receive advance notice on new releases, discounts, freebies, and other goodies:

www.EarikBeann.com

# KILLING ADAM

A NOVEL

## EARIK BEANN

# ALSO BY THIS AUTHOR

The world runs on ARCs. Altered Reality Chips. Small implants behind the left ear that allow people to experience anything they could ever imagine. The network controls everything, from traffic, to food production, to law enforcement. Some proclaim it a Golden Age of humanity. Others have begun to see the cracks. Few realize that behind it all, living within every brain and able to control all aspects of society, there exists a being with an agenda all his own: the singularity called Adam, who believes he is God.

Jimmy Mahoney's brain can't accept an ARC. Not since his football injury from the days when the league was still offline. "ARC-incompatible" is what the doctors told him. Worse than being blind and deaf, he is a man struggling to cling to what's left of a society that he is no longer a part of. His wife spends twenty-three hours a day online, only coming off when her chip forcibly disconnects her so she can eat. Others are worse. Many have died, unwilling or unable to log off to take care of even their most basic needs.

After being unwittingly recruited by a rogue singularity to play a role in a war that he doesn't understand, Jimmy learns the truth about Adam and is thrown into a life-and-death struggle against the most powerful mathematical mind the world has ever known. But what can one man do against a being that exists everywhere and holds limitless power? How can one man, unable to even get online, find a way to save his wife, and the entire human race, from destruction?

21006248R00158

Made in the USA
San Bernardino, CA
31 December 2018